LANGUAGE ALCHEMY

Bridging the Gap Between Humans and Machines Through Language

Lillian Synthia

TABLE OF CONTENTS

Introduction

It is introducing "Language Alchemy: Bridging the Gap Between Humans and Machines Through Language," an insightful e-book that explores the fantastic world of language and how it can change how people interact with machines. In this digital age, where technology is advancing at an unprecedented pace, the convergence of human communication and artificial intelligence has become a focal point of exploration.

This e-book's pages untangle the complex web of language as an alchemical transformation catalyst, acting as the link between two seemingly unrelated realms. It is more precise and straightforward to us as we negotiate the complex terrain of human-machine interaction that language is more than just a means of communication; instead, it is a powerful force determining our shared future.

The trip starts with a history of language's development and an explanation of its crucial function in human society. We unearth the layers of linguistic development that have prepared the way for the mutually beneficial partnership between humans and machines, from ancient civilizations to the digital era. The e-book explores how language, once the exclusive domain of humans, is now a medium through which engines comprehend and respond to our complex expressions.

Venturing into artificial intelligence, we examine the mechanisms that enable machines to understand and generate language. This e-book clarifies the principles and algorithms underpinning natural language processing, illuminating the complexities of converting unprocessed data into meaningful communication.

In addition, "Language Alchemy" considers the moral implications of this linguistic synthesis, discussing the difficulties and possibilities that emerge as machines become increasingly ingrained in our daily lives. As we strive for a harmonious coexistence between humans and machines, the transformative potential of language appears as a guiding principle, facilitating understanding, collaboration, and innovation in this dynamic intersection of technology and humanity.

Explore language as the alchemical spark that connects us to the artificial intelligence of the future as you go on a fascinating journey. "Language Alchemy" beckons you to ponder the profound implications of this linguistic journey, inviting readers to envision a future where the synthesis of human and machine communication transcends boundaries and propels us into a new era of collective intelligence.

Chapter I

Foundations of Language

Historical Development of Language

The foundation of human communication, language, has a complex and multi-thousand-year history. The interaction of cultural, social, and cognitive elements has woven a complex tapestry of language evolution. The purpose of this section is to examine how historically language by following its beginnings, significant events, and changes that have molded the varied linguistic environment that exists now.

Researchers and academics continue to disagree about the origins of language. Several theories try to explain how language originated, but they are only sometimes accepted. One prominent theory suggests that language evolved gradually, starting with primitive vocalizations and gestures among early Homo sapiens. These primitive means of communication evolved into increasingly complex means of expression, providing the groundwork for language as we know it today.

Proto-languages, or early linguistic systems, first appeared in the prehistoric era. These languages were ancestors of the wide variety of languages spoken today. Small populations said proto-languages, which separately developed in various locations. As these communities grew and interacted, linguistic diversity flourished, giving rise to distinct language families.

An important turning point in the evolution of language history was the invention of writing. Writing systems were independently developed by ancient civilizations, including Mesopotamia, Egypt, and China, in order to record information, communicate, and pass on knowledge to future generations. Scripts such as Cuneiform, Hieroglyphics, and Logographics demonstrate how prehistoric people encoded language into written form. Not only did writing help preserve historical and cultural tales, but it also helped standardize languages within particular areas.

Language has always been essential in forming and characterizing cultural identities. Languages became indicators of diverse communities as civilizations grew, giving speakers a sense of community. The linguistic diversity observed in ancient Greece, where different city-states developed unique dialects, exemplifies how language became intertwined with regional and cultural distinctions.

Along with facilitating the flow of goods, the Silk Road network of trade routes also promoted the cross-pollination of languages between East and West. As merchants, travelers, and scholars traversed this vast network, tongues mingled, leading to linguistic borrowings, adaptations, and the enrichment of vocabularies. This interconnection significantly influenced the history of languages, which also promoted linguistic diversity and cultural hybridity.

Religious books, including the Bible, Quran, and Vedas, have greatly influenced language growth and preservation. These holy texts functioned as archives of grammatical constructions, lexical diversity, and linguistic forms. Religious scriptures were translated into many languages, which helped to standardize and codify language, guaranteeing its survival and impact on future generations.

The Renaissance witnessed a resurgence of interest in classical languages, particularly Latin and Greek. Viewing historical languages and literary traditions as sources of inspiration for thought and culture, scholars and humanists worked to bring them back to life. This renewed focus on classical languages influenced linguistic norms, educational practices, and the development of grammatical rules that shaped modern languages.

The historical evolution of languages bears the permanent imprint of colonialism. Native languages were frequently displaced and marginalized as a result of European powers imposing their languages on colonial countries in their desire for worldwide dominance. Due to the significant effects of this linguistic imperialism, creole languages—which combined aspects of the colonizer's language and regional vernaculars—came into being.

Technological advancements that transformed communication were among the revolutionary societal shifts brought about by the Industrial Revolution. People could communicate quickly and over great distances thanks to the telegraph, telephone, and, eventually, the internet, which broke down communication barriers based on language and location. Technological progress had an impact on language by hastening the spread of linguistic trends, dialectal changes, and the creation of new vocabulary linked to industrial and scientific breakthroughs.

The 20th century saw linguistics undergo unparalleled growth, propelled by cognitive science, anthropology, psychology, and linguistics breakthroughs. Noam Chomsky revolutionized our understanding of language learning with his idea of Universal Grammar, which postulated that language acquisition is an underlying human tendency. This change in viewpoint opened up new study directions by encouraging further investigation into the cognitive underpinnings of language.

Globalization, characterized by increased interconnectedness and cultural exchange, has led to the rise of lingua francas—languages that serve as common means of communication among speakers of different native languages. English has become the de facto language, particularly in education, international business, and diplomacy. This phenomenon of language use illustrates how dynamic language is and how it may change to meet the changing demands of a world that is becoming more interconnected.

Throughout human civilization, language has undergone a fascinating historical development. From the rudimentary vocalizations of early Homo sapiens to the globalized linguistic landscape of the 21st century, language has evolved as a dynamic and integral aspect of human culture and communication. Knowing this evolution helps us to understand language's complexity, plasticity, and resilience—a timeless example of how human expression is constantly changing.

Language's Influence on Human Societies

The foundation of human communication, language, profoundly impacts the social structures of all cultures and historical periods. This section explores how language maintains, reflects, and shapes human communities. Language is a mirror and a catalyst, shaping civilizations from the finer points of interpersonal communication to the more expansive domains of culture, politics, and identity. By navigating the complex relationship between language and culture, we can uncover the significant influence that linguistic dynamics have had throughout human history.

Fundamentally, language is a cultural artifact that represents a community's collective identity, beliefs, and customs. Language is a tool that societies use for myth-making, storytelling, and passing down cultural legacy to future generations. Language becomes a living archive of a society's past, serving as a thread of narrative that unites people within a familiar cultural setting. The richness of vocabulary, idioms, and metaphors encapsulates the essence of cultural nuances, allowing a community to express its unique worldview and perspectives.

Linguistic diversity is woven throughout human communities like a tapestry. Languages exist on all continents and within all nation-states in many forms, each reflecting the historical, geographical, and social conditions in which they originated. A mosaic of identities is fostered by linguistic diversity, which allows people to express their unique experiences and viewpoints. Yet, this diversity is not without its challenges, as linguistic differences can also become markers of social hierarchies, contributing to linguistic discrimination and inequality within societies.

In the process of creating and negotiating social identity, language is essential. Accents, dialects, and linguistic markers all serve as potent symbols that people use to convey their membership in particular social groupings. Sociolinguistics examines how linguistic decisions reflect and shape social roles, class distinctions, and cultural affinities to create identities. The intersectionality of language and identity highlights the dynamic and malleable character of social classifications impacted by linguistic subtleties.

Politics and language interaction is a complicated and frequently acrimonious field. States and other political organizations understand how effective language can be in maintaining a feeling of national identity and cohesion. Political goals can be provided with by language laws that support a national language or stifle minority languages. On the other hand, linguistic activism works to protect and revive endangered languages while opposing the forces of political power that homogenize them.

Many societies still feel the effects of colonization in their language landscapes. Colonizers imposed their languages on indigenous populations, often marginalizing local languages and eroding cultural identities. In post-colonial cultures, the lingering vestiges of colonial languages serve as reminders of past oppression, demonstrating the lasting impact of linguistic imperialism.

Reclaiming indigenous languages, appreciating their inherent worth, and opposing the linguistic hierarchy imposed by colonial history are all part of decolonization.

Language is a compelling economic instrument that affects international relations, trade, and commerce. The importance of some languages—like Mandarin and English—in international business and diplomacy highlights the effects of linguistic dynamics on the economy. The correlation between economic prospects and the ability to speak a widely recognized language creates linguistic hierarchies that worsen social and economic inequalities. The pursuit of linguistic capital, or the strategic use of language skills for financial gain, further underscores the economic dimensions of language within societies.

The digital era has revolutionized communication across societies through technology, leading to the emergence of new linguistic forms and expression methods. In addition to hastening language spread, social media platforms, instant messaging, and digital communication have brought in new linguistic norms and vernaculars. As a global communication network, the internet has facilitated linguistic exchange, creating a virtual space where languages evolve, borrow, and adapt at an unprecedented pace.

The dynamic force of language is what propels societal transformation. Language is a powerful tool that social movements and advocacy campaigns frequently use to disrupt social conventions, increase awareness, and galvanize populations. New terminologies and inclusive language are linguistic developments that reflect changing societal attitudes and further the conversation on environmental sustainability and gender equality. Language's capacity to transform and spark social change emphasizes its agency in determining the future paths that civilizations will take.

Language transmission, standardization, and perpetuation depend heavily on education. Language acquisition, literacy, and educational policies shape linguistic landscapes. The advancement of multilingualism, the availability of various linguistic resources, and the caliber of education influence how people acquire and use language in individuals and societies. Education becomes a key battleground for linguistic preservation, as the choices made in curricula and language policies influence the vitality of languages within the educational sphere.

Globalization, characterized by increased interconnectedness and interdependence, has resulted in two outcomes: it has encouraged linguistic diversity and standardized language usage. While global communication allows for the exchange of languages and cultural expressions, the dominance of a few international languages threatens the survival of more minor languages. The sustainability of languages in a world growing more interconnected by the day is called into question by the conflict between the pressures of globalization and the preservation of linguistic diversity.

In conclusion, language has a significant, diverse, and always-changing impact on society. From its role as a cultural keystone and identity marker to its entanglement with politics, economics, and technology, language shapes the very essence of human interactions.

Cultures continue to manage the intricate relationships between linguistic dynamics and social structures, demonstrating language's power to alter the past, present, and future. Comprehending the intricacies of this association is crucial in cultivating inclusiveness, conserving linguistic heterogeneity, and maneuvering through the obstacles and prospects posed by the mutually beneficial tango between language and society.

The role of language in shaping social interactions is evident in the establishment and maintenance of social hierarchies. Language's subtleties—such as tone, intonation, and word choice—help convey the power structures in a community. Language-based formality, informality, and politeness indicators can tell social standing and either support or contradict preexisting standards. People's language choices in social interactions reflect and reinforce society's ideals, impacting the establishment and maintenance of relationships.

Cohesive human societies are founded on the unbreakable bond between language and cultural identity. Language is a primary vehicle through which cultural values, traditions, and narratives are passed on from generation to generation. Community members develop a feeling of identity through dialects, idioms, and linguistic subtleties. Maintaining and advancing linguistic diversity adds to the diverse fabric of world cultures and extends our knowledge of the shared human experience.

The relationship between language and power is a recurrent theme in shaping human societies. People who control the narrative, whether in politics, the media, or educational settings, significantly influence societal norms and the way the public thinks. Language can uplift or subjugate people, affecting their perceptions of others and themselves. Efforts to promote linguistic inclusivity and challenge linguistic biases are integral to fostering equitable and inclusive societies as they strive to amplify diverse voices and perspectives.

Language as a Cultural Phenomenon

Language is an intricate and dynamic communication system closely entwined with human cultures' cultural fabric. Language is more than just a means of communication ideas and thoughts; it also plays a significant role in reflecting and shaping society. This section examines the complex interrelationships between language and culture, focusing on how language shapes social norms, expresses cultural identity, and serves as a shared knowledge base. Understanding language as a cultural phenomenon offers us a new perspective on the diversity and richness of human communities.

Fundamentally, language is a cultural creation shaped by a people group's customs, history, and shared experiences rather than an objective instrument. Idioms, syntax, and vocabulary of languages all reflect the cultural contexts in which they originated. Diverse languages frequently capture distinct worldviews, exposing the concepts, values, and priorities important to society. For example, the depth with which some languages can convey the complexities of nature or family dynamics reflects the significance of these elements within the respective cultures.

Language has a strong cultural identity and is a linguistic marker to separate different communities. Accents, dialects, and linguistic subtleties serve as emblems of identity and as tools for communication. People's speech patterns, word selections, and colloquial idioms represent their cultural upbringing. Language is a potent tool for creating and preserving group identity because it strengthens social ties and promotes a sense of community.

The variety of linguistic environments found worldwide proves positive of the cultural importance of language. The thousands of languages spoken globally reflect the geographic distribution of human populations and mirror the diversity of cultures that have shaped them. Each language represents a unique repository of cultural knowledge, containing the stories, myths, and histories that define a particular community. Therefore, the erasure of a distinct way of knowing and interpreting the world is involved in losing a language, making it more than a linguistic occurrence.

Cultural nuances embedded in language extend beyond vocabulary, including communication styles, politeness norms, and conversational rituals. Significant cultural differences exist in the value of non-verbal cues, the acceptance of silence as a communication technique, and the use of formal or informal addresses. For instance, whereas some cultures value directness and evident verbal expression, others may favor indirect communication and subtly transmit meaning through gestures. Understanding these cultural subtleties is crucial for effective intercultural communication and building cross-cultural relationships.

As a cultural phenomenon, language is essential in creating and maintaining social norms and reflecting them. Within a society, linguistic expressions can sustain power relations, social hierarchies, and gender roles. For example, gendered language may promote assumptions and preconceptions about what it means to be a man or a woman. Social norms can be upheld or challenged by how language frames social roles. This could affect perceptions, behaviors, and expectations. Bilingualism and multilingualism are excellent examples of how language and culture interact.

People who traverse various linguistic and cultural contexts have a sophisticated comprehension of the relationship between language and cultural identity. Bilingualism is the ability to communicate in many languages while navigating the social mores and cultural peculiarities specific to each language. Bicultural people are frequently more aware of when language use is appropriate in a given environment and adjust their language repertoire accordingly.

Language and culture studies have always been at the core of linguistics. Ethnolinguistics is a subfield of linguistics that focuses on the relationship between language and culture, significantly how social conventions and cultural values shape language. The Sapir-Whorf hypothesis, put out by linguists like Edward Sapir and Benjamin Lee Whorf, postulates that a language's lexicon and structure can constrain and mold speakers' cognitive processes, affecting how they understand and classify the outside world. There is recognition of the impact language can have on cognitive processes and cultural viewpoints, even though the strong version of this idea has drawn criticism.

The cultural phenomena of language are dynamic and ever-changing, adapting to the demands of the society in which it is utilized. Introducing new concepts, technologies, and social dynamics necessitates linguistic adaptation. New terms, or neologisms, are created to express innovative ideas and show how culture is constantly changing. Furthermore, languages frequently absorb vocabulary and idioms from one another, particularly in multiethnic and multilingual communities, illustrating how linguistic barriers are brittle and porous.

The continuity and preservation of cultural legacy depend heavily on language's function in cultural transmission. Oral traditions, storytelling, and folklore passed down through generations contribute to the information of cultural knowledge. In many cultures, language serves as a sacred vessel that conveys historical wisdom, morals, and mythology in addition to being a medium of communication. The preservation of indigenous languages is essential to preserving distinctive cultural viewpoints that could otherwise disappear in the face of globalization.

Written language becomes a storehouse of cultural accomplishments and accumulated wisdom. Literature, poetry, and religious texts capture the essence of a culture, providing insights into its worldview, moral values, and aesthetic sensibilities. Shakespeare's plays, for instance, are cultural relics that give insight into the Elizabethan era in addition to being literary masterpieces. Sacred books like the Bible, Vedas, or Quran are not only religious texts; they are also priceless linguistic and cultural artifacts that influence the customs and beliefs of entire societies.

The impact of dominant languages on the international scene in today's interconnected globe poses concerns regarding linguistic imperialism and the preservation of linguistic variety. English is the universal language essential to worldwide trade, science, and diplomacy. Although knowing English helps one access opportunities and information worldwide, it also raises concerns about the possible loss of linguistic diversity. Efforts to promote multilingualism and preserve endangered languages are essential for maintaining the richness of the linguistic mosaic that characterizes human cultural expression.

The nexus between language and culture has expanded with the advent of the digital age. Social media platforms, online content creation, and digital communication tools have transformed how language is used and disseminated. Hashtags, memes, and emojis have become cultural symbols that transcend linguistic barriers, creating a

globalized digital culture. However, there are drawbacks to the digital sphere, like the quick dissemination of false information and the possible standardization of language and cultural expression.

Chapter II

The Digital Revolution and
Linguistic Evolution

The Digital Age: Catalyst for Linguistic Transformation

The advent of the digital age has ushered in an era of unprecedented technological advancements, fundamentally transforming how individuals communicate, share information, and interact with the world. Language, a dynamic and adaptable instrument that has experienced significant changes in response to the opportunities and difficulties posed by digital technology, is at the center of this digital revolution. This section investigates the various ways in which the digital era has sparked linguistic change. It does this by looking at the influence of digital communication platforms, the development of language in virtual environments, and the effects of these changes on communication dynamics and the expression of culture.

Digital communication platforms, from social media networks to instant messaging applications, have become integral to contemporary life. These platforms have not only altered the speed and scale of communication but have also given rise to new linguistic norms and conventions. The brevity imposed by character limits on platforms like Twitter, for instance, has led to the emergence of abbreviations, acronyms, and other forms of linguistic compression. This shift towards concise and efficient communication reflects the demand for quick, easily digestible information in the digital landscape.

The emergence of emoticons and emojis is another significant linguistic change made possible by the digital era. In a time when most communication occurs through screens instead of face-to-face contact, these visual symbols convey emotions and nuances that can be lost in written text. Emojis are currently seen as a universal language that bridges linguistic divides and offers a more inclusive and expressive form of communication. Their widespread use in digital discourse highlights how language may change to accommodate new forms of human communication.

The proliferation of linguistic diversity has been further stimulated by digital technology using the globalization of communication. Mainly, social media makes it possible for people with different language origins to converse with each other on a worldwide level. The digital world's melting pot of languages, dialects, and cultural expressions promotes a dynamic linguistic ecology. Translation tools and multilingual platforms further contribute to this linguistic diversity, enabling users to communicate and share content in their preferred languages.

But language is affected by the digital era in ways beyond written and spoken communication. Voice-activated technologies, such as virtual assistants and smart speakers, have introduced a new dimension to human-computer interaction. These gadgets can comprehend and respond to spoken language thanks to natural language processing algorithms, which obfuscate the distinction between human and computer communication. Creating conversational agents that can understand context, tone, and intent is becoming essential to language evolution in the digital era as people increasingly converse with artificial intelligence.

The internet, a pillar of the digital age, has created new language genres and modes of expression in addition to facilitating the global spread of information. For instance, memes are becoming a common way to express satire, humor, and cultural commentary. Frequently disseminated virally, these textual and visual artifacts show how language is collaborative and participatory in the digital sphere. Memes rely on shared cultural references and an implicit understanding of online communities, highlighting the role of the internet in shaping unique linguistic subcultures.

The digital age has also witnessed the emergence of a new form of language—code. As programming languages become essential tools for creating digital applications and systems, a growing population engages with coding languages to navigate and manipulate the digital world. Although code may not look like spoken or written language, it is a means of communication for computers, influencing how people interact with and perceive the digital world. Coding in multiple languages has become critical, demonstrating how language evolves outside human contact.

Social media, in particular, has profoundly impacted the evolution of language in the digital age. People can share ideas, stories, and artistic expressions with a worldwide audience on social media sites like Facebook, Instagram, and TikTok. Social media's immediacy and connectivity facilitate the quick dissemination of linguistic trends, resulting in a faster evolution of the digital vernacular. Online challenges, linguistic memes, and hashtags serve as platforms for linguistic innovation and serve as a window into the collective imagination of internet users.

The digital age has also witnessed the rise of user-generated content platforms, such as blogs, vlogs, and podcasts. These platforms enable people to express themselves and their stories in various languages. Due to the democratization of content creation, there are now many different voices, dialects, and cultural expressions available in the digital sphere. Bloggers and content creators use language not only as a means of communication but as a tool for storytelling, advocacy, and cultural representation.

There are difficulties associated with language evolution in online environments. Concerns about the quality of online discourse, the dissemination of false information, and the possible deterioration of linguistic standards have arisen with the advent of the digital age. Specific digital platforms favor brevity, which can result in oversimplification and the loss of subtlety in communication. Furthermore, the quick distribution of material online—often without enough verification—can aid in propagating grammatical errors and misunderstandings.

The digital age has also given rise to the phenomenon of digital dialects and online subcultures. Online communities create jargon, slang, and comedy, frequently based on shared beliefs, hobbies, or fandoms. These digital dialects serve as markers of group identity, making a sense of belonging among community members. The rise of memes, acronyms, and internet jargon unique to particular online subcultures emphasizes how language is dynamic and changes to meet the special communication needs of digital groups.

In addition to linguistic innovations, the digital age has introduced new ethical considerations surrounding language use. In the digital sphere, problems, including hate speech, online abuse, and the propagation of extreme ideologies, have gained significant attention. Online platforms' anonymity can encourage people to use destructive language, making it difficult for societies to balance allowing people to express them freely and preventing harm in the digital sphere.

The impact of the digital age on language goes beyond textual communication to encompass audio-visual communication as well. The rise of video-sharing platforms like YouTube and streaming services has given individuals the means to communicate through spoken language, gestures, and visual storytelling. The shift in content types from long-form, conventional videos to short-form material, such as vlogs and micro-content, demonstrates how these platforms impact language. People can now express themselves in many linguistic and cultural ways because of the democratization of visual communication brought about by the accessibility of video-making tools.

Incorporating machine learning and artificial intelligence into digital communication has ushered in a new era of language automation. Chatbots, language translation services, and predictive text features all use these technologies to enhance and speed up communication processes. Although these developments are practical and efficient, they also raise concerns about the possible standardization of language and the effect of automation on linguistic subtlety and inventiveness.

The definition of literacy has also changed in the digital age beyond knowing how to read and write. Digital literacy encompasses navigating, critically evaluating, and creating content in digital environments. The changing nature of communication in the digital age, where people must navigate a vast and linked web of information, is reflected in the shift in literacy needs. The ability to decipher and engage with diverse forms of digital content, including multimedia and interactive platforms, has become an integral aspect of contemporary literacy.

Social Media's Impact on Language Dynamics

Social media, ubiquitous in the digital landscape, has redefined how individuals communicate, share information, and construct their digital identities. This profound shift in communication dynamics has inevitably left its mark on language, transforming linguistic norms, fostering new modes of expression, and influencing the evolution of communication styles. This section explores the multifaceted impact of social media on language dynamics, examining the role of platforms such as Facebook, Twitter,

Instagram, and TikTok in shaping linguistic innovation, discourse patterns, and the construction of online communities.

The brevity imposed by character limits on platforms like Twitter has given rise to linguistic compression, leading to the emergence of abbreviations, acronyms, and other forms of shorthand. The need to convey information concisely within the constraints of limited characters has spurred linguistic creativity, giving birth to new words and expressions. This language economy on Twitter, defined by the skill of distilling ideas into brief but powerful tweets, has influenced other digital communication channels and made communication more streamlined and effective.

Emojis and emoticons, graphical representations of emotions and expressions, have become integral to social media communication. These visual symbols serve as a non-verbal layer that complements written text, allowing users to convey emotions, tone, and context in a concise and universally understood manner. The proliferation of emojis transcends linguistic barriers, creating a visual language that enhances the emotional richness of online communication. Emojis contribute to establishing a common visual lexicon among many linguistic communities and adding nuance to text-based communications.

Initially a simple metadata tag, the hashtag has evolved into a powerful linguistic tool on social media platforms. Hashtags organize content, facilitate discovery, and unite individuals around shared interests. The hashtag has evolved from an organizing tool to a vehicle for activism, humor, and expression. By making particular language patterns more visible, hashtags foster a lively, interactive environment where users can influence the direction of online conversation. The hashtag movement that has gained widespread traction reflects the communal nature of language creation in the digital era.

The visual nature of platforms like Instagram and TikTok has altered the way individuals construct narratives and communicate. Memes, videos, and pictures have emerged as popular forms of expression that impact the online platform's visual lexicon. Combining visual and textual elements allows users to convey complex ideas and emotions in a multimodal format. Memes are a kind of comedy, satire, and criticism of culture that help build standard cultural references among members of online communities.

Social media has also given rise to a phenomenon known as "internet slang" or "netspeak." This informal and playful form of language includes abbreviations, acronyms, and linguistic innovations characteristic of online discourse. New idioms frequently appear and spread quickly inside online forums, resulting in the rapid evolution of internet slang. Using internet slang creates a sense of in-group identity among users who share a common digital culture, reinforcing the idea that language on social media is not static but constantly evolving.

Linguistic innovation on social media extends to creating neologisms—newly coined words or expressions. Memes, viral challenges, and online trends contribute to the rapid circulation and adoption of new vocabulary. These language innovations frequently come from user-generated material and are incorporated into more extensive online conversations. The fluidity of language on social media reflects the adaptability of communication in the digital age, where linguistic trends can emerge, gain traction, and evolve at a pace unparalleled in traditional forms of communication.

The participatory nature of social media platforms, where users actively engage with content and contribute to discussions, has democratized linguistic expression. Users become co-creators of content, influencing linguistic trends through likes, shares, comments, and the creation of user-generated content. This participatory aspect of social media communication challenges traditional notions of linguistic authority, highlighting the role of the community in shaping language dynamics.

The immediacy of social media communication has also influenced the temporality of language. Because internet conversation is brief, linguistic trends can quickly emerge, peak, and decrease. This rapid turnover of linguistic phenomena, from viral expressions to trending hashtags, creates a dynamic linguistic environment where novelty and relevance drive language use. The transience of linguistic trends on social media contrasts the enduring nature of language evolution in more traditional contexts.

Social media has introduced a new dimension to language variation, where geographic factors, digital communities, and subcultures influence linguistic diversity. Online communities form around shared interests, hobbies, fandoms, or ideologies, creating linguistic microcosms within the broader digital landscape. The unique linguistic codes, slang, and expressions developed within these communities become markers of group identity, reinforcing a sense of belonging among members.

Social media has encouraged linguistic diversity and innovation but has also sparked worries about the caliber of online conversation. Character restrictions encourage brevity, which, when paired with the hurried pace of social media conversations, can cause communication to become overly simplistic and lose its subtlety. The ease with which information spreads online can contribute to the rapid dissemination of linguistic inaccuracies, misinformation, and the perpetuation of harmful linguistic behaviors.

Social media platforms, as conduits for global communication, have brought attention to issues related to language standardization and linguistic imperialism. The dominance of English on many social media platforms can contribute to linguistic homogenization, potentially sidelining the linguistic diversity of non-English-speaking communities. Promoting multilingualism and linguistic inclusivity on social media is essential for addressing these concerns and fostering a more equitable digital linguistic landscape.

Integrating artificial intelligence and machine learning algorithms in social media platforms introduces a new layer to language dynamics. These algorithms, designed to curate content based on user preferences, engagement patterns, and linguistic analysis, play a role in shaping the content that users encounter. The implications of algorithmic curation on language exposure, linguistic diversity, and the formation of online echo chambers raise essential questions about the impact of technology on the linguistic environments individuals inhabit on social media.

Language use and the creation of digital identities on social media are closely related. Individuals curate their online personas through linguistic choices, tone, and the content they share. The juxtaposition of visual elements with textual content allows users to present a curated version of themselves, contributing to the performative nature of online communication. The language used on social media becomes a tool for self-expression, identity construction, and the negotiation of social roles within digital spaces.

Internet English: A Linguistic Subculture

The Internet has created a linguistic subculture known as "Internet English," which consists of a specific collection of idioms, customs, and communication methods that are different from those found in traditional forms of English. Numerous online environments, such as social media sites, forums, chat rooms, and online gaming communities, have been affected by this language problem. Memes, emojis, internet slang, and the participatory nature of online interactions and digital subcultures have all formed the dynamic and ever-evolving form of communication known as Internet English. This section delves into the traits, development, and cultural relevance of Internet English, illuminating its function as a unique linguistic subculture within the larger context of the English language.

Internet English differs from formal or traditional versions of English in several linguistic ways. One noteworthy feature is the usage of internet slang, a compilation of acronyms, abbreviations, and lighthearted idioms that have developed inside online communities. Terms like "LOL" (laugh out loud), "BRB" (be right back), and "OMG" (oh my God) have become ubiquitous in digital communication, reflecting a desire for brevity and informality in online interactions. Internet slang is a means of efficient communication within the constraints of digital platforms and a form of linguistic innovation that fosters a sense of belonging among Internet users.

Another essential component of Internet English is emojis and emoticons, which provide a visual and emotional dimension to written communication. Users may concisely and widely communicate emotions, tone, and context using smiley faces, thumbs up, and other pictorial symbols. Emojis have evolved into a universal language that can assist in creating a shared visual language in digital contexts and communicate across linguistic barriers. Emojis are a deviation from conventional textual communication conventions; they highlight the significance of non-verbal clues in the digital sphere.

The participatory nature of online platforms has fueled the rapid evolution of Internet English. Users actively contribute to developing linguistic trends through likes, shares, and comments, creating a collaborative and dynamic linguistic environment. Memes, a form of Internet humor often in the form of images with text, play a significant role in shaping Internet English. Memes encapsulate cultural references, societal critiques, and spirit, serving as linguistic artifacts that are shared, adapted, and remixed across various online communities. The viral nature of memes contributes to spreading and adopting specific linguistic expressions, creating a sense of cohesion among internet users.

The Internet has given rise to a practice called "copypasta," in which a passage of text is copied and pasted into numerous online communities and forums. These textual repetitions frequently take the shape of ludicrous claims, fables, or funny anecdotes. Copypasta is a language meme that spreads quickly and changes as users alter the words to suit various situations. This form of linguistic repetition reflects Internet English's collaborative and iterative nature, where linguistic elements are recycled and repurposed creatively.

The linguistic subculture of Internet English is not limited to written communication; it extends to spoken language in the form of Internet memes and catchphrases that find their way into everyday conversation. Phrases like "epic fail," "facepalm," and "I can't even" have become part of the broader cultural lexicon, transcending their origins in online spaces. Internet English's ubiquity in offline communication highlights its cultural relevance and impact on language use outside the digital sphere.

Online gaming communities represent a unique subset within the linguistic landscape of Internet English. Gamers often generate a unique lexicon of acronyms, slang, and idioms specific to the gaming community. Terminologies particular to gaming, such as "noob" (a newbie), "GG" (excellent game), and "nerf" (to undermine a game element), have permeated larger online conversation. Online gaming's collaborative and competitive features encourage the development of a common language, strengthening the sense of community among participants.

With their worldwide and varied user base. Platforms like Twitter's character limits promote the usage of acronyms and abbreviations, which improve communication efficiency and brevity. Originally intended as a metadata tool, hashtags have developed into a language expression medium that helps organize content into categories and fosters the growth of online communities centered around shared interests or concerns. Social media's linguistic features, including hashtags, mentions, and retweets, have become integral to the communicative norms of Internet English.

Internet English's ability to adjust and change with the times is demonstrated by how it handles linguistic difficulties and societal shifts. For instance, a new set of linguistic terms and acronyms about the virus and public health measures emerged due to the COVID-19 epidemic. Words like "work from home," "social distancing," and "quarantine" proliferated in online conversation, demonstrating how Internet English is constantly adapting to shared experiences and world events.

However, the impact of Internet English extends beyond linguistic innovation; it influences broader communication norms and cultural expression. The informality and playfulness of Internet English challenge traditional notions of formal written communication. People can now express themselves authentically on online platforms by utilizing unusual linguistic elements in more formal contexts. This change in communication standards is especially noticeable in digital environments that encourage originality, creativity, and authenticity.

The linguistic subculture of Internet English also raises questions about language standardization and the coexistence of multiple linguistic varieties. While some argue that Internet English lowers language norms, others view it as a dynamic and innovative form of communication that reflects the evolving nature of language. The tension between linguistic innovation and standardization is not new, but the digital age has intensified this debate as Internet English becomes more prominent in public discourse.

The cultural significance of Internet English lies in its role as a marker of digital identity and community affiliation. The linguistic features and expressions used in online spaces contribute to constructing individual and collective identities. Online communities, defined by shared interests, ideologies, or fandoms, develop their linguistic codes and norms, creating a sense of belonging among members. Adopting specific linguistic elements allows individuals to signal their affiliation with online subcultures.

However, the rapid evolution of Internet English also poses challenges, especially regarding inclusivity and accessibility. Using acronyms, memes, and internet slang might provide linguistic difficulties for people who need to learn more about the online culture. This begs whether online communities include all users or if individuals needing help with English on the Internet might need to be included. Initiatives to address language proficiency and computer skills gaps are necessary to promote a more inclusive online environment.

Chapter III

Challenges and Opportunities in a Globalized Digital Landscape

Linguistic Diversity in the Digital World

The digital age has brought an unprecedented level of connectedness, which has changed how people interact, share information, and communicate. As the internet connects people across geographic boundaries, it becomes a dynamic space where languages and cultures converge. Linguistic diversity, a hallmark of human expression, takes on new dimensions in the digital world. This section explores the complex link between linguistic diversity and the digital realm, focusing on how the digital sphere challenges and enriches the wide variety of worldwide languages.

The internet, as a global network, has the potential to bridge linguistic divides and facilitate cross-cultural communication. However, the prevalence of several languages—English foremost among them—raises questions regarding linguistic imperialism and the possible loss of linguistic diversity. English, as the lingua franca of the internet, is a dominant medium for online content, leading to the marginalization of non-English languages. This linguistic hierarchy challenges speakers of less widely spoken languages, navigating a digital landscape where English often takes center stage.

Multilingualism is being promoted to address linguistic gaps on the internet and tools for localization and translation are being created. Platforms that support multiple languages, such as social media networks and search engines, play a crucial role in fostering linguistic diversity. Artificial intelligence-driven translation systems enable information transfer across linguistic barriers, increasing the accessibility of digital content for users of different languages. These efforts contribute to a more inclusive digital environment that reflects the richness of the world's linguistic tapestry.

The digital age's ubiquitous force, social media, becomes a microcosm of linguistic diversity. Individuals with varying linguistic origins participate in online groups, exchange content, and have conversations. However, there are drawbacks to this linguistic diversity. The character limits imposed by platforms like Twitter can influence language use, encouraging using abbreviations and linguistic shortcuts. Furthermore, language hurdles may arise for individuals unfamiliar with online communities' standard cultural references due to the quick spread of memes and internet slang. While social media enhances linguistic diversity by providing a platform for various languages, it also introduces linguistic adaptation and understanding complexities.

A potent tool for celebrating and preserving linguistic diversity is digital storytelling. Through online channels, people and communities can exchange stories, customs, and cultural expressions in their original tongues. Blogs, podcasts, and digital content creation allow for exploring linguistic nuances and representing diverse voices. The democratization of content creation in the digital world empowers speakers of minority languages to assert their linguistic identity and contribute to the global narrative.

Language revitalization efforts find new avenues in the digital age. Endangered and minority languages facing the threat of extinction can leverage digital technologies to document, teach, and revitalize linguistic traditions. Online language courses, language learning apps, and digital repositories become tools for preserving linguistic heritage. Indigenous communities, in particular, utilize digital platforms to share oral traditions, document endangered languages, and connect with a global audience. Thus, the digital world triggers the revival of languages that are in danger of going extinct.

The digital landscape, however, has challenges to linguistic diversity. The dominance of major technology companies, often based in English-speaking regions, influences the development and accessibility of digital tools. This dominance may cause linguistic features that benefit speakers of less widely spoken languages to be overlooked. The lack of linguistic diversity in the design of digital interfaces, voice recognition systems, and virtual assistants can lead to exclusion and hinder the full participation of diverse linguistic communities in the digital sphere.

The rise of user-generated content introduces a new layer to linguistic diversity in the digital world. Online communities, forums, and discussion platforms become spaces where individuals express themselves in their native languages. Linguistic codes, slang, and expressions specific to particular digital subcultures evolve within these communities, creating a vibrant and dynamic linguistic ecosystem. This diversity in online discourse reflects the plurality of voices in the digital landscape and challenges the notion of a homogenized, globalized language.

The digital age has also given rise to a phenomenon known as "digital dialects." Online groups frequently based on shared interests or subcultures have their linguistic terms and conventions. Internet memes, catchphrases, and linguistic novelties emerge within these communities, creating unique digital dialects. The shared linguistic codes within digital subcultures serve as markers of group identity, fostering a sense of belonging among community members. Digital dialects' malleability and fluidity mirror language's ability to change online.

Online spaces become crucibles for language contact and the evolution of hybrid linguistic forms. The interplay of languages within digital communities leads to the creation of code-switching, a phenomenon where individuals seamlessly switch between languages within a single conversation. This fluidity highlights the dynamic nature of language in the digital age and questions conventional ideas of linguistic purity. Multiple languages coexisting in online discourse foster linguistic diversity and provides a forum for linguistic identity negotiation.

Digital activism has become potent in advocating for linguistic rights and inclusivity. Online campaigns, hashtags, and social media movements amplify the voices of linguistic minorities, drawing attention to issues of language preservation, revitalization, and recognition. The digital world provides a platform for linguistic advocacy, allowing communities to connect, collaborate, and mobilize globally. Digital activism becomes a tool for challenging linguistic inequalities and promoting the rights of speakers of all languages, regardless of their global prominence.

The digital world also challenges traditional linguistic boundaries, blurring distinctions between languages and creating new forms of communication. A "diglossic" reality, where people move between formal, standardized languages and the informal, dynamic languages of the digital sphere, is the result of the growth of a transnational digital culture. The fusion of languages in online spaces creates a hybrid linguistic landscape, challenging traditional notions of linguistic purity and stability.

The impact of artificial intelligence (AI) on language use in the digital world introduces a new dimension to linguistic diversity. Natural language processing algorithms and machine translation technologies influence how individuals interact with digital content. The standardization of language by AI systems can reduce linguistic diversity, as algorithms prioritize certain language varieties over others.

Online Language Communities: Opportunities and Challenges

The introduction of the internet has fundamentally altered the ways in which people interact and communicate with one another on a global scale. Online language communities, virtual spaces where users interact, share information, and engage in discourse using a particular language or set of languages, have emerged as vibrant hubs of linguistic diversity and cultural exchange. These virtual communities present exceptional chances for acquiring language skills, discovering different cultures, and establishing international relationships. However, they also raise issues regarding online discourse norms, language authenticity, and the possibility of echo chambers. This section investigates the diverse terrain of virtual language groups, examining the prospects they offer and the difficulties they create in the ever-changing digital world.

Online language communities serve as valuable platforms for language learning and cultural exchange. Regardless of geographical location, language learners can immerse themselves in authentic linguistic environments, interacting with native speakers and honing their language skills. Language exchange forums, social media groups, and dedicated language-learning apps allow users to connect with speakers of their target language, fostering a sense of community and shared learning experiences because these collaborative platforms enable a safe space where people may ask questions, practice having conversations, and learn about subtle cultural differences.

One of the critical advantages of online language communities is their accessibility to a wide array of languages. Users can investigate languages that aren't usually taught in conventional classrooms or need more resources for mass teaching. This inclusivity enables the preservation and promotion of less widely spoken languages, contributing to linguistic diversity in the digital realm. Additionally, members of linguistic minority cultures can locate online networks celebrating their languages, giving them a sense of empowerment and affirmation.

Social media platforms, in particular, significantly shape online language communities. Facebook groups, Twitter threads, and Instagram accounts dedicated to specific languages or language families create digital spaces where users share linguistic insights, discuss language-related topics, and celebrate cultural expressions. The immediacy and interconnectedness of social media facilitate real-time communication and foster a sense of belonging among language enthusiasts. Hashtags about language acquisition and diversity serve as focal areas for community interaction, enabling users to find and establish connections with like-minded people worldwide.

On the other hand, there are disadvantages to virtual language communities and opportunities that need to be adequately evaluated. One notable challenge is the issue of linguistic authenticity. In online spaces, users may encounter a range of language proficiency levels, and the quality of language use may vary. The informal digital communication style, typified by linguistic shortcuts, online slang, and abbreviations, can occasionally deviate from accepted linguistic conventions. This begs the issue of how informal online discourse affects language acquisition and how nonstandard language variants might spread.

The potential for echo chambers within online language communities is another challenge. Users frequently look for communities that support their cultural interests or language learning objectives, creating close-knit communities where conventions are upheld for language use and shared viewpoints. Although these communities foster a sense of community, they may also restrict access to a broader range of linguistic expressions, cultural views, and dialects. Striking a balance between the comfort of a supportive community and the need for exposure to linguistic diversity becomes a delicate consideration for online language learners.

Reducing linguistic disparities is another issue that online language communities must deal with. The dominance of specific languages, mainly English, in online spaces can marginalize non-English languages. Platforms and communities primarily operating in English may inadvertently exclude speakers of other languages, reinforcing linguistic hierarchies. To address these disparities and develop a digital landscape that represents the linguistic diversity of its users, multilingualism and inclusive language-learning settings are essential.

Another consideration is the potential for cultural appropriation and the commodification of languages within online communities. Languages and artistic expressions are sometimes reduced to commodities for consumption, divorced from their historical and social contexts. Language learning apps, for example, may prioritize popular languages based on market demand, perpetuating the notion that specific languages are more valuable or desirable than others. Striking a balance between fostering language learning opportunities and respecting the cultural significance of languages is essential to ensure ethical engagement within online language communities.

The gamification of language learning, facilitated by various apps and platforms, introduces opportunities and challenges. While gamified language learning can enhance user engagement and motivation, it may also need to be more concise in language acquisition and pay more attention to the depth and complexity of linguistic and cultural understanding. The emphasis on quick wins and point-based systems can create a superficial approach to language learning, potentially hindering users from gaining a deeper appreciation for the cultural and historical aspects of their study languages.

Artificial intelligence (AI) technologies began to appear inlanguage learning apps and online communities introduces new dimensions to the digital language landscape. AI-powered chatbots and online language instructors provide individualized learning experiences by adjusting to the needs of each user. While these technologies enhance accessibility and provide additional resources for language learners, they also raise questions about the impact of automation on human connection and the authenticity of language interactions. Balancing the advantages of AI-driven language learning tools with the preservation of human connection and cultural understanding remains a critical consideration for the future of online language communities.

The dynamic character of virtual language communities necessitates a sophisticated comprehension of the changing interplay among language, technology, and cross-cultural communication. Digital spaces provide opportunities for the democratization of language learning, enabling individuals from diverse backgrounds to access resources, connect with native speakers, and celebrate linguistic diversity. However, to fully harness the potential of online language communities, stakeholders, including educators, technology developers, and community organizers, must address the challenges related to linguistic authenticity, inclusivity, and the ethical implications of language commodification.

Efforts to promote linguistic diversity within online language communities should prioritize the inclusion of less widely spoken languages and recognize linguistic minority communities. Language learning platforms and apps can proactively support the documentation and preservation of endangered languages, collaborating with linguists and community members to create resources that contribute to language revitalization efforts. By fostering partnerships with speakers of diverse languages, online language communities can become catalysts for preserving linguistic heritage.

Language educators also play a crucial role in shaping the landscape of online language communities. They can leverage digital platforms to create inclusive and culturally responsive learning environments, acknowledging the linguistic diversity of their students. Incorporating diverse language varieties, cultural references, and real-world communication scenarios into online language courses enhances the authenticity of language learning experiences. Educators can guide students in critically engaging with digital resources, encouraging them to explore languages beyond the curriculum and promoting a more nuanced understanding of linguistic diversity.

Balancing Global Connectivity with Linguistic Preservation

One of the key characteristics that distinguishes our globally interconnected environment in the quickly changing 21st century is global connectedness. The rise of the internet, social media, and digital communication platforms has facilitated unprecedented interactions among people from diverse linguistic and cultural backgrounds. While this connectivity brings immense opportunities for collaboration, understanding, and shared knowledge, it raises critical questions about the impact on linguistic diversity and the preservation of less widely spoken languages. This section examines the difficult balancing act between language preservation and global connectedness, highlighting the opportunities, risks, and moral dilemmas involved in doing so.

The digital age has ushered in an era of unparalleled global connectivity, enabling individuals to communicate and collaborate across borders with unprecedented ease. People from various linguistic backgrounds come together virtually on social media platforms, messaging apps, and online forums, fostering cross-cultural communication. In this age of digital agora, English frequently acts as a universal language, facilitating communication between speakers of many original tongues. This universal language promotes worldwide communication but raises questions about the possible standardization of speech and the loss of linguistic diversity.

One of the primary challenges posed by the dominance of English in online communication is the potential marginalization of non-English languages. Because English is the primary language used for digital platforms, content, and services, speakers of other languages could find it challenging to navigate a linguistic environment where their perspectives are less prevalent. The digital divide, where access to information, educational opportunities, and resources is frequently biased in favor of English speakers, is exacerbated by this linguistic hierarchy on the internet. This imbalance needs to be corrected to build a more equitable digital world that reflects the linguistic diversity of the world's people.

Global connectedness presents a dilemma because it can protect and undermine language diversity. On the one hand, linguistic heritage can be celebrated and preserved via the internet. Social media groups, forums, and online language communities turn into places where speakers of less common tongues can interact, exchange resources, and build a feeling of community. Through technology, communities can utilize the digital sphere to document and revitalize endangered languages, thereby contributing to language preservation. However, linguistic minorities may face pressure to adapt or integrate due to the widespread use of English as the primary language on the internet, which could result in the marginalization of their native tongues.

Efforts to balance global connectivity with linguistic preservation involve the promotion of multilingualism in digital spaces. Platforms and services can implement language localization features, allowing users to interact in their native languages. Machine translation technology can help with cross-language communication by removing language barriers and promoting inclusivity. Search engines, social media platforms, and online content providers are essential in fostering an atmosphere that fully engages people speaking different languages in the digital conversation. Furthermore, programs that encourage the production of digital material in lesser-spoken languages help to build an online environment that is more inclusive and diverse in terms of language.

Linguistic preservation in the digital age also relies on the collaboration between technology developers, linguists, and language communities. Language documentation projects leverage digital tools to record, archive, and share linguistic resources, including dictionaries, grammar, and audiovisual materials. Communities can develop digital archives of their languages via mobile apps and web platforms, giving future generations access to a priceless resource. Technology professionals and linguists working together make it easier to create tools tailored to the particular requirements of different languages, which helps preserve and revitalize linguistic heritage.

Social media's advent has dramatically impacted how people use and retain language. Tongues are utilized on social media sites such as Facebook, Instagram, and Twitter for advocacy, communication, identity-building, and cultural expression. Hashtags, social media difficulties, and trends all contribute to linguistic phenomena that show how language is dynamic in the digital age. Users of less widely spoken languages can express their linguistic identities, debunk linguistic misconceptions, and interact with a global audience through the interactive elements of social media. Social media has thus evolved into a tool for language empowerment and a platform for expressing numerous linguistic viewpoints.

Nonetheless, despite increased global connectivity, linguistic preservation continues to encounter difficulties. Social media's emphasis on immediacy, brevity, and viral content can cause language to become too simplified and distorted. Internet slang, abbreviations, and the pressure to conform to dominant linguistic norms influence how speakers of less widely spoken languages express themselves online. The quest for likes, shares, and visibility may inadvertently lead to the dilution of linguistic richness in favor of more widely understood or trendy language forms. Striking a balance between linguistic diversity and digital communication demands remains an ongoing challenge for language communities navigating the digital landscape.

The international diffusion of digital media, such as music, literature, and films, also influences language dynamics. Digital platforms provide prospects for fostering cultural and linguistic variety, yet they also present cultural appropriation and commercialization obstacles. Lesser-spoken languages risk being isolated from their cultural and historical backgrounds and treated like strange objects to be consumed. The commercialization of languages within the digital space raises ethical questions about linguistic and cultural diversity representation, highlighting the need for responsible and respectful engagement with less widely spoken languages.

The role of education is paramount in addressing the challenges posed by global connectivity to linguistic preservation. Promoting multilingualism, linguistic appreciation, and cultural sensitivity is a crucial responsibility of educational institutions, language educators, and legislators. Integrating digital literacy programs into language education can empower students to navigate the digital landscape critically and engage with diverse linguistic content. Digital technologies for language learning should be included in language curriculum to ensure that students are prepared to take advantage of the opportunities provided by the digital age while also considering the moral issues surrounding linguistic diversity.

Digital storytelling emerges as a potent tool for supporting and maintaining language variety. Online forums allow people and groups to exchange oral histories, cultural expressions, and language narratives. Digital storytelling projects, including podcasts, blogs, and online videos, become tools for documenting languages, allowing communities to showcase the richness and uniqueness of their linguistic heritage. Storytelling creates an emotional connection, fostering a deeper appreciation for each language's cultural and linguistic nuances.

Understanding cultural sensitivity, respect, and cooperation is necessary to weigh the ethical implications of maintaining language preservation while promoting global connectedness. Digital platforms, content creators, and users all play a role in shaping the digital language landscape. Content moderation policies should be designed with cultural diversity in mind, avoiding the imposition of linguistic norms that may perpetuate linguistic inequalities. To provide inclusive features, address concerns about cultural appropriation, and guarantee that digital spaces respect and celebrate linguistic diversity, platforms should actively cooperate with linguistic communities.

Chapter IV

Language Technology:
From Theory to Practice

Fundamentals of Natural Language Processing (NLP)

Natural Language Processing (NLP) is the discipline that integrates artificial intelligence, computer science, and linguistics to enable machines to understand, interpret, and produce human language in a meaningful and contextually relevant way. This can lead to various applications, such as sentiment analysis, information retrieval, chatbots, and language translation. Understanding NLP's roots requires examining the key components, approaches, and challenges that define this dynamic field.

At its core, NLP involves the development of algorithms and models that empower machines to process and understand human language in a manner analogous to how humans do. Pre-processing textual input is the first stage in natural language processing (NLP). This includes procedures like stemming, which reduces words to their most basic form, and tokenization, which separates sentences into distinct words or tokens. These preparatory steps lay the groundwork for subsequent analyses and applications.

One of the main functions of natural language processing (NLP) is part-of-speech (POS) tagging, in which each word in a sentence is assigned a specific grammatical category, such as noun, verb, adjective, or adverb. Syntactic analysis, which entails comprehending the grammatical structure of phrases, depends on POS tagging. Syntactic parsing, another critical NLP task, goes beyond POS tagging by determining the relationships between words and their hierarchical structure within a sentence, resembling how humans parse and understand penalties.

Beyond syntactic analysis, NLP encompasses semantic analysis, aiming to discern the meaning of words, phrases, and entire sentences. One of the most critical tasks in semantic analysis is word sense disambiguation (WSD), which tackles the problem of interpreting a word with numerous meanings depending on the context in which it is used. Another component that concentrates on determining the roles of various things within a sentence, such as the subject, object, or predicate, is semantic role labeling.

One widespread use of NLP is machine translation, the automatic translation of text between languages. Two essential methods in this field are statistical and neural machine translation. While neural machine translation uses deep neural networks to grasp complex linguistic relationships and subtleties, resulting in more accurate translations, statistical machine translation depends on statistical models that learn translation trends from vast bilingual corpora.

Sentiment analysis, or opinion mining, represents another facet of NLP where algorithms analyze text to determine the sentiment expressed—positive, negative, or neutral. Sentiment analysis finds applications in customer reviews, social media monitoring, and market research, providing valuable insights into public opinion and sentiment trends.

Named Entity Recognition (NER) is a critical NLP task involving identifying and classifying entities, such as names of people, organizations, locations, dates, and other specific elements within a text. Text summarization and question-answering systems are two applications that benefit from NER's essential work in information extraction and knowledge representation.

One excellent illustration of how NLP may be applied to enhance human-computer interactions is the rise of conversational agents or chatbots. Chatbots read user input, provide relevant responses, and conduct natural language conversations using natural language processing (NLP) techniques. These apps go beyond basic rule-based frameworks, integrating machine learning algorithms that allow chatbots to pick up on and adjust to user interactions gradually.

NLP has made incredible strides, yet the field still faces many obstacles. Because words and phrases can have different meanings depending on the situation, ambiguity in language presents a severe challenge. It is necessary to use sophisticated models with contextual awareness to address this ambiguity. Another challenge is language diversity, which encompasses numerous dialects, slang phrases, and everyday idioms. For NLP models to be applicable in real-world contexts, they need to be adjusted to consider this heterogeneity.

The cultural and linguistic diversity of global languages introduces additional complexities. NLP models trained on a particular language may struggle to generalize across languages with distinct linguistic structures and nuances. This challenge is particularly pronounced in languages with limited digital resources and data, hindering the development of robust NLP applications for these languages.

Ethical considerations also come to the forefront in NLP, especially concerning bias in language models. Models trained on biased datasets may perpetuate and amplify societal biases, leading to unfair or discriminatory outcomes. Addressing discrimination in NLP models requires a concerted effort to curate diverse and representative datasets and implement ethical guidelines in developing and deploying NLP applications.

The advent of deep learning has significantly influenced the landscape of NLP. In many NLP tasks, deep neural networks—particularly transformer models and recurrent neural networks (RNNs)—have shown unmatched performance. Since their introduction by Vaswani et al. in the paper "Attention is All You Need," transformers have grown to be the foundation of cutting-edge models such as GPT (Generative Pre-trained Transformer) and BERT (Bidirectional Encoder Representations from Transformers). These models' ability to collect contextual information and long-range relationships through employing attention mechanisms accounts for their efficacy in tasks such as language interpretation, translation, and text generation.

Pre-trained language models are a recent development in natural language processing (NLP) that entails training models on large text corpora and then optimizing them for particular tasks. Models are helpful in various applications because of this pre-training, which makes it possible for them to capture general linguistic knowledge and patterns. The transferability of pre-trained models has sped up NLP research by enabling developers and researchers to expand on pre-existing language representations for various language tasks.

NLP has reached new heights thanks to deep learning, but there are drawbacks, especially regarding processing power and the necessity for large labeled datasets. Ample transformer model training requires significant computer power, prohibiting smaller research groups or teams from participating. In addition, the requirement for large datasets for model training raises privacy concerns, making data collection, use, and storage crucial.

Few-shot and zero-shot learning have become popular study topics in NLP in recent years. These methods are intended to improve the generalization of the models by allowing them to execute tasks with little or no task-specific training samples. This is in line with creating language models that are more flexible and adaptive so they can perform well in a range of language-related tasks without requiring a lot of task-specific training.

In the domain of NLP, the idea of Explainable AI (XAI) has gained popularity, particularly as models get more complicated. Understanding and interpreting the decisions made by NLP models are critical for their deployment in real-world applications. XAI approaches seek to explain model predictions, build confidence in AI systems, and offer clear and understandable insights into the inner workings of language models.

Looking ahead, the future of NLP holds exciting possibilities and challenges. Multimodal NLP integrates language understanding with other modalities, such as images and audio, and is an emerging area with applications in fields like image captioning, video analysis, and accessibility technologies. Furthermore, the investigation of contextual embeddings—words embedded according to the context of a sentence—keeps improving language representations, making models better at capturing linguistic subtleties and nuances.

With the creation of approachable tools and platforms, NLP is becoming more accessible, and more people are becoming involved in the discipline. People with different experiences and specialties can contribute to and profit from advances in language technology as NLP becomes more widely available. Cooperative projects and open-source initiatives enable the production of shared resources, datasets, and benchmarks, promoting innovation and advancement in natural language processing.

Algorithms and Models in NLP

The goal of the multidisciplinary discipline of natural language processing (NLP), which sits at the nexus of computer science, linguistics, and artificial intelligence, is to enable machines to comprehend, interpret, and produce human language. A fundamental aspect of NLP is designing and implementing algorithms and models that empower machines to process language in a way that resembles human comprehension. This section explores the ideas and techniques underlying natural language processing (NLP), including their history, uses, and problems they try to solve.

In the early days of NLP, statistical approaches were pivotal in addressing language-related tasks. These methods used statistical models to find patterns and connections in big-text corpora. One notable application was machine translation, where statistical models learned the probabilities of word sequences in one language corresponding to sequences in another. Although these models showed promise, they needed to help understand context and interpret the language's finer points.

Rule-based systems are an example of an early NLP technique where linguistic patterns and rules were manually created to enable robots to understand and interpret language. These systems relied on predefined rules, often created by linguists and language experts, to analyze and generate language. Although rule-based systems offered an organized approach to address particular linguistic issues, they needed help adjusting to natural language's complexity and intrinsic unpredictability.

NLP underwent a dramatic change with the introduction of machine learning, which brought data-driven methods capable of automatically identifying patterns in samples. A popular paradigm in natural language processing (NLP) is supervised understanding, which entails training models on labeled datasets so they may discover correlations between input data (text, for example) and matching output labels (sentiment, for example). Support Vector

Machines (SVMs), decision trees, and Naive Bayes classifiers were early machine learning algorithms applied to NLP tasks.

One of the most transformative developments in NLP has been integrating neural networks and deep learning. The capacity of recurrent neural networks, or RNNs, to capture sequential dependencies, were early pioneers in this domain. However, the breakthrough came with the introduction of transformer models, as exemplified by the seminal work on BERT (Bidirectional Encoder Representations from Transformers) and GPT (Generative Pre-trained Transformer). These models, characterized by attention mechanisms and deep architectures, demonstrated remarkable success in various NLP tasks.

One significant development in NLP is word embeddings, which involve expressing words as vectors in a continuous vector space. Models like Word2Vec, GloVe (Global Vectors for Word Representation), and FastText contributed to the development of word embeddings. By capturing the semantic relationships between words, these embeddings enable algorithms to recognize contextual similarities and contrasts. Word embeddings have become foundational for various NLP applications, including sentiment analysis, document clustering, and information retrieval.

Sequence-to-sequence models, enabled by the encoder-decoder architecture, have become instrumental in machine translation and text summarization tasks. Models like the Transformer architecture facilitated the generation of coherent and contextually rich sequences by processing input sequences (e.g., source language sentences) and generating output sequences (e.g., translated sentences). Attention mechanisms in these models allow them to focus on different input parts when developing each output piece.

Transfer learning, a paradigm that involves training models on a source task and fine-tuning them for a target task, has become a cornerstone of recent NLP advancements. Pre-trained models like BERT and GPT are trained on large text corpora to learn general language representations. These trained models can be modified for specific downstream tasks, allowing one to show how available language understanding knowledge can be used for task-specific applications.

Despite advancements, NLP algorithms still need help. One of the biggest obstacles in language is ambiguity, which occurs when words or sentences have different meanings depending on the context. Resolving this ambiguity requires models that can understand contextual clues and nuances. The diversity of language, which includes many dialects, slang terms, and everyday idioms, presents another difficulty. Adapting models to handle this variability is crucial for their effectiveness in real-world scenarios.

The task of Named Entity Recognition (NER) entails identifying and categorizing entities in a text, including names of individuals, groups, places, dates, and other particular features. Even though deep learning has significantly advanced NER, problems with identifying entities in many languages and contexts still need to be solved. Furthermore, managing uncommon or invisible entities presents a constant difficulty.

The deployment of NLP models raises ethical considerations, especially concerning bias. Models trained on biased datasets may perpetuate and amplify societal biases, leading to unfair or discriminatory outcomes. Addressing discrimination in NLP models requires careful curation of diverse and representative datasets and the implementation of ethical guidelines in model development and deployment.

A developing field in NLP is the integration of several modalities, including text, pictures, and audio. Multimodal natural language processing (NLP) integrates data from various sources to improve language comprehension. Video analysis, image captioning, and accessibility technologies are some examples of applications. The challenges in multimodal NLP include developing models that can effectively fuse information from different modalities to derive meaningful insights.

As NLP models become increasingly complex, the need for Explainable AI (XAI) becomes crucial. Understanding and interpreting the decisions made by NLP models are critical for their deployment in real-world applications. XAI techniques aim to provide transparent and interpretable insights into the inner workings of language models, offering explanations for model predictions and fostering trust in AI systems.

Looking ahead, the future of NLP holds exciting possibilities and challenges. Continued advancements in deep learning, including exploring novel architectures and training techniques, will likely refine language representations further. More involvement and creativity are being encouraged by the democratization of NLP, which is facilitated by creating approachable tools and platforms. NLP advances more quickly due to cooperative and open-source projects that create shared resources, datasets, and benchmarks.

Ethics in Language Technology: A Consideration

The field of language technology, which includes many applications, including machine translation, speech recognition, and natural language processing, or NLP, is playing a bigger role in determining our communication, information-gathering, and digital system interactions. As these technologies advance, ethical considerations become paramount, demanding scrutiny of the impact on individuals, communities, and societies. This section explores the multifaceted ethical dimensions associated with language technology, addressing concerns related to bias, privacy, linguistic diversity, and the responsible deployment of these powerful tools.

One of the foremost ethical concerns in language technology revolves around explicit and implicit bias in algorithms and models. Preferences present in the data may be unintentionally learned and reinforced by language models trained on big datasets. This is particularly true for machine learning models trained on internet data, which could include socioeconomic, racial, and gender stereotypes, among other cultural prejudices. Biased language technology can exacerbate already-existing disparities by producing discriminating results. For instance, biased sentiment analysis algorithms may reinforce stereotypes, while machine translation systems may propagate cultural or gender biases. Addressing bias in language technology requires concerted efforts in data curtain, algorithmic design, and ongoing evaluation to ensure fair and equitable outcomes.

To preserve the diversity of languages and the cultural settings they reflect, language technology must carefully traverse the complex terrain of linguistic diversity. While major languages often receive substantial attention, linguistic minorities, and less widely spoken languages may face marginalization in the development of language technologies. Due to its potential to undermine language diversity and cultural heritage, this linguistic disparity presents ethical questions. Efforts to promote inclusive language technology involve the development of resources for diverse languages, including datasets, models, and tools. Collaborative initiatives that engage with linguistic communities and prioritize documenting and preserving endangered languages contribute to a more ethically grounded approach to language technology.

The widespread adoption of language technology, particularly in voice-activated virtual assistants, speech recognition, and language processing applications, raises significant privacy concerns. These technologies gather and process voice data, which is frequently private and sensitive, endangering user privacy. The accidental recording of private conversations, the storage of voiceprints, and the potential for unauthorized access to voice data raise ethical questions about user consent, data ownership, and the responsible use of personal information. Moral language technology development requires robust privacy policies, transparent data handling practices, and mechanisms for informed user consent to mitigate potential privacy infringements.

A key component of using language technology ethically is ensuring informed permission. Users must understand how their language data is gathered, used, and processed. Transparent communication regarding the capabilities and limitations of language technologies empowers users to make informed decisions about their engagement with these systems. Furthermore, empowering users with authority over their data—including the ability to erase data and adjust privacy settings—improves user agency. The ethical imperative lies in fostering an environment where individuals are aware of the implications of using language technology and have the tools to actively shape their digital interactions in ways that align with their values and preferences. When language technology is used without due thought, unexpected outcomes can occur. One example is when language models produce objectionable or dangerous content.

The use of automated text production to spread false information. The possibility of hostile assaults that alter language technology behavior.

Ethical development practices involve incorporating safeguards and countermeasures to mitigate these unintended consequences. Frequent evaluations, observation, and timely resolution of new moral quandaries facilitate the conscientious advancement of language technology.

Ensuring accessibility and inclusivity in language technology is an ethical imperative. Digital communication and information access should be inclusive for individuals with diverse linguistic abilities, including those with speech or language disorders. Accessibility-focused language technologies improve the chances for people with disabilities to participate actively in digital platforms. The ethical dimension of inclusivity extends to the design of user interfaces, the availability of assistive technologies, and the commitment to removing barriers that may impede equal access to language technology benefits.

The development of language technology also brings about ethical issues surrounding the propagation of misinformation and manipulation. Text generation models can fabricate news items, mimic people, and produce misleading material. Our moral duty is to create technologies with built-in systems to identify and lessen the effects of misinformation. Technological solutions, user education, and cooperative efforts with other stakeholders, such as media organizations and fact-checking projects, are needed to mitigate the harmful societal effects of manipulated language technology.

An overarching ethical consideration in language technology revolves around the principle of human-centric AI. Ensuring that AI systems, including language technologies, serve humanity's best interests requires prioritizing ethical design principles. Human values, human rights, and coordinating AI development with social welfare are all part of human-centric AI. Ethical frameworks should guide the responsible use of language technology, emphasizing accountability, transparency, and the continual assessment of societal impact to prevent the unintended reinforcement of harmful biases or the creation of technology that undermines human values.

Language technology, when deployed globally, necessitates cross-cultural sensitivity. Nuances in language use, cultural references, and linguistic expressions vary across different regions and communities. Ethical considerations involve avoiding cultural appropriation, stereotyping, or misrepresentation in language technology applications. Language technologies respect and reflect the various linguistic and cultural settings in which they are used by working in partnership with linguists, communities, and specialists in diverse cultures. Striking a balance between global applicability and cultural sensitivity is crucial for the ethical deployment of language technology worldwide.

Ethical considerations begin at the research and development stage of language technology. Researchers and developers are responsible for conducting ethically sound research, ensuring the fair representation of diverse voices in datasets, and considering the potential societal impact of their work. Experts from linguistics, ethics, and cultural studies work together in collaborative, multidisciplinary settings to create more ethically sound and comprehensive development processes.

Promoting ethical behavior in language technology requires education and awareness initiatives. Users, developers, and policymakers should be informed about the ethical considerations associated with language technologies. Talks on bias reduction, privacy protection, and the appropriate use of language technology should all be included in educational programs. Fostering a culture of ethical awareness within the language technology community and society at large is essential for ensuring a responsible and conscientious approach to developing and deploying these technologies.

Developing robust regulatory frameworks and industry standards is instrumental in ensuring ethical practices in language technology. When creating policies that address privacy, fairness, accountability, and transparency in the use of language technology, governments, industry players, and regulatory organizations are essential. These frameworks should develop with technological advances to tackle new ethical dilemmas. Industry collaboration and adherence to ethical standards contribute to the responsible growth of language technology and the protection of user interests.

Chapter V

Human-Machine Interaction Through Language

Virtual Assistants and Chatbots: The Linguistic Bridge

Chatbots and virtual assistants have ushered in a new era of human-computer interaction and fundamentally altered how people engage with technology. Rooted in Natural Language Processing (NLP) and artificial intelligence, these linguistic interfaces bridge users and digital systems, facilitating seamless communication through natural language. The section explores the evolution, applications, linguistic intricacies, and impact of virtual assistants and chatbots, examining their role as linguistic bridges that enhance accessibility, convenience, and efficiency in diverse domains.

The roots of virtual assistants and chat bots trace back to early attempts to create conversational agents. Eliza, developed in the 1960s, marked one of the earliest instances of a chatbot simulating a Rogerian psychotherapist through simple pattern matching. Nevertheless, the expansion of the internet and developments in machine learning and natural language processing allowed significant strides in the subject. The introduction of Siri in 2011 and the subsequent releases of Google Assistant, Amazon Alexa, Microsoft Cortana, and others demonstrated the assimilation of virtual assistants into commonplace technology. Simultaneously, chatbots proliferated on social media, messaging apps, and websites, serving various purposes.

In customer service, chatbots provide instantaneous responses to frequently asked queries, freeing up human workers to handle trickier issues. E-commerce platforms use virtual assistants to improve the buying experience by providing tailored advice and support. Chatbots facilitate symptom checking, appointment scheduling, and medication reminders in healthcare. Educational chatbots support learning through interactive conversations, while in finance, virtual assistants assist with banking transactions, budgeting, and financial advice. These illustrations show how chatbots and virtual assistants can improve accessibility and efficiency across various industries.

At the heart of virtual assistants and chatbots lies their linguistic prowess, enabled by sophisticated NLP algorithms. These systems generate and comprehend language similar to that of humans by using a variety of NLP approaches. Tokenization, syntactic analysis, and semantic processing form the foundation for learning user inputs. Using sentiment analysis, virtual assistants can better understand the emotional tone of user messages and respond with empathy and appropriate context. Named Entity Recognition (NER) makes identifying entities from user queries possible, which promotes more precise and pertinent interactions. The continuous evolution of NLP models, such as transformers, has significantly enhanced the linguistic capabilities of virtual assistants, enabling them to engage in more natural and context-aware conversations.

Virtual assistants and chatbots' user experiences are greatly influenced by conversational design. When creating natural, intuitive, and user-friendly interactions, linguistic considerations must be carefully considered. They are creating conversational flows, creating virtual assistant personas, and taking user input into account, all of which help to develop conversational interfaces that are both interesting and useful. The objective is to build a smooth language bridge that considers user preferences, expectations, and cultural quirks. The success of virtual assistants and chatbots hinges on their linguistic accuracy and their ability to create a positive and frictionless conversational experience.

Chatbots and virtual assistants have made incredible progress in language comprehension, but they continue to confront difficulties. Context-dependent meanings, ambiguity in language, and different linguistic styles hamper accurate interpretation. Slang, regional dialects, and colloquial expressions add layers of complexity. Resolving these challenges requires ongoing advancements in NLP, incorporating diverse linguistic datasets, and adapting to the evolving nature of language use. Striking a balance between linguistic flexibility and precision remains a crucial challenge for developers aiming to enhance the linguistic capabilities of these conversational agents.

The linguistic bridge constructed by virtual assistants and chatbots extends across linguistic boundaries, necessitating support for multilingual interactions. Accommodating diverse languages, dialects, and variants requires robust language models to comprehend and generate content in multiple languages. Moreover, cross-cultural sensitivity is imperative to ensure that virtual assistants respect cultural norms, avoid unintentional biases, and adapt to the linguistic nuances of different user groups. The task involves offering multilingual assistance and cultivating a linguistically diverse atmosphere that mirrors the worldwide diversity of customers.

Linguistic bridges that work well are sensitive to users' unique preferences and contextual subtleties. Virtual assistants and chatbots increasingly incorporate personalization features to tailor responses based on user history, preferences, and behavior. Contextual awareness involves understanding the flow of a conversation, referencing past interactions, and adapting responses to the immediate context. Achieving personalized and contextually aware conversations demands sophisticated NLP models that can discern user intent, track conversation history, and dynamically adjust linguistic outputs to enhance the user experience.

Deploying virtual assistants and chatbots raises ethical considerations concerning user privacy, consent, and the responsible use of linguistic data. Conversations with virtual assistants often involve sensitive information, requiring stringent measures to safeguard user privacy. Transparency in data handling practices, clear communication about data usage policies, and mechanisms for user consent are essential ethical considerations. Moreover, avoiding manipulating users through persuasive linguistic techniques and ensuring that virtual assistants respect ethical guidelines in healthcare and counseling are critical aspects of responsible linguistic interactions.

The trajectory of virtual assistants and chatbots points towards continual evolution, driven by advancements in linguistic technologies and user-centric design. Future developments may witness even more sophisticated NLP models that transcend language barriers, better understand user emotions, and navigate complex linguistic contexts. Multimodal interfaces, integrating text with speech and visual elements, represent a frontier for enhancing the richness of linguistic interactions. Explainable AI (XAI) in language interfaces is expected to alleviate user concerns about accountability and transparency in virtual assistant decision-making.

Voice-Activated Devices: Shaping Conversations

The introduction of voice-activated gadgets has completely changed how people interact with technology and represents a paradigm shift in human-computer interaction. Driven by sophisticated speech recognition and natural language processing (NLP) technologies, these gadgets have increased in contemporary homes, seamlessly integrating into everyday activities. Voice-activated technologies, from smart home appliances and in-car systems to virtual assistants such as Apple's Siri and Amazon's Alexa, have become powerful tools in influencing human-machine dialogue. This section explores the evolution, linguistic intricacies, applications, challenges, and societal impact of voice-activated devices, delving into their role as catalysts for more natural and accessible human-computer conversations.

Voice-activated gadgets have their origins in the early 20th-century attempts to recognize speech. The early systems needed more vocabulary and processing capability, making them crude. However, the area saw a revolution with the introduction of neural networks and deep learning. The development of robust automatic speech recognition (ASR) systems allowed devices to accurately transcribe spoken words, forming the foundation for effective voice-activated interactions. Concurrent advances in natural language processing (NLP) enabled machines to comprehend and react to natural language queries, paving the way for increasingly complex and context-aware dialogues.

The revolutionary power of voice-activated gadgets is rooted in the language nuances of these technologies. Thanks to NLP approaches, these gadgets can understand the subtleties of human language, such as syntax, semantics, and context. Speech-to-text conversion, a fundamental aspect of these devices, involves translating spoken words into text, demanding accurate recognition of phonetic patterns and language models that capture syntactic structures. Natural language understanding (NLU) allows devices to decipher spoken queries into meaningful information, grasp human intent, and sense sentiment. With the ongoing development of language models like transformers, voice-activated machines may now converse more naturally, contextually richly, and human-like thanks to their enhanced linguistic capabilities.

Voice-activated gadgets have become ubiquitous, enhancing human-machine dialogue in many contexts. In virtual assistants, devices like Amazon's Alexa, Google Assistant, and Apple's Siri serve as digital companions, offering assistance with tasks ranging from setting reminders and sending messages to providing weather updates and controlling smart home devices. Voice-activated systems improve automobile driving safety by allowing hands-free communication, entertainment, and navigation. Smart home devices, from thermostats to lighting systems, respond to voice commands, fostering a seamless and intuitive user experience. These uses highlight the adaptability of voice-activated gadgets and establish them as essential elements of today's technology environment.

The linguistic customization features of voice-activated devices greatly enhance the user experience. Because these gadgets can distinguish between different voices, user interactions can be tailored according to context, history, and preferences. Linguistic personalization is adjusting suggestions, actions, and replies to each user's linguistic preferences and habits. Users thus enjoy a more customized and intuitive experience, which builds a sense of familiarity and improves the general use of voice-activated gadgets. The ability of these gadgets to function as tailored assistants that recognize and meet each user's specific language needs is demonstrated by linguistic personalization.

Despite their extraordinary powers, Voice-activated gadgets have speech detection and understanding limitations. Accent, dialect, and speech pattern variations make it difficult to record and comprehend speech accurately—ambiguities in language, including homophones and context-dependent meanings, present challenges in understanding user intent. Robust speech recognition and understanding require models that can adapt to diverse linguistic inputs, learn from user feedback, and continually evolve to encompass the richness and variability of natural language. To guarantee that voice-activated devices provide inclusive and efficient linguistic interactions for users with varying linguistic backgrounds and preferences, it is imperative to tackle these problems.

The evolution of voice-activated devices extends beyond speech recognition, encompassing the development of multimodal interfaces that integrate speech with visual and contextual elements. Intelligent displays, augmented reality, and responsive graphical interfaces complement voice interactions, providing users with a richer and more immersive experience. Multimodal interfaces extend the linguistic bridge, enabling users to combine speech with gestures, taps, and visual cues for a more nuanced and flexible interaction. This convergence of modalities improves usability and accessibility, especially when combined visual and aural feedback provides a more complete user experience.

Voice-activated gadgets have a profound social influence that affects inclusion, accessibility, and the democratization of technology. Voice-activated devices are a breakthrough for impaired people because they provide an interface beyond conventional input methods. Voice interfaces empower those with mobility impairments, visual challenges, or conditions affecting fine motor skills to navigate digital environments, access information, and control devices independently. The increased accessibility facilitated by voice-activated devices contributes to a more inclusive digital landscape, reducing barriers and ensuring that technology is accessible to individuals with diverse abilities.

Voice-activated gadgets are becoming more commonplace, bringing up ethical and privacy issues. Voice data, often containing sensitive information, is processed and stored by these devices. Privacy breaches, accidental recordings, and unauthorized access to voice data pose potential risks. Transparency in data management procedures, informed user consent, and user control and deletion tools for voice data are all ethical factors. Robust privacy policies, ethical development processes, and continuous attempts to address emerging ethical concerns in this fast-evolving domain must balance the ease of voice-activated interactions and the requirement to safeguard user privacy.

New developments that promise to improve language interactions further define the direction that voice-activated gadgets will go in the future. Continued advancements in ASR and NLP models will refine these devices' accuracy and contextual understanding. Combining sentiment analysis and emotion identification will allow gadgets to sense and react to human emotions, enabling emotionally intelligent dialogue. Furthermore, voice-activated devices are expected to play a significant role in the healthcare sector, allowing uses such as remote patient monitoring, mental health assistance, and prescription administration. Furthermore, the exploration of natural language generation (NLG) in voice responses holds the potential to make interactions even more dynamic and contextually relevant.

Language and Artificial Intelligence Integration in Everyday Life

Artificial intelligence (AI) and language integration are being interwoven into our daily lives because of technology's rapid and ever-changing nature. Language, the cornerstone of human communication, has undergone a transformative journey with the infusion of AI, reshaping how we interact, learn, and navigate the world around us. The complex relationship between language and AI integration is examined in this article, along with its significant effects on communication, education, personal support, and the ethical issues raised by this paradigm shift in technology.

The combination of artificial intelligence and language technologies has significantly impacted communication, an essential human function. In this trend, the development of natural language processing, or NLP, has allowed machines to understand, interpret, and produce language akin to that of humans. Natural language processing (NLP) is used in the real world to improve communication through chatbots, virtual assistants, and language translation services. These AI-powered solutions promote a more cohesive global society by enabling smooth communication across language and cultural divides. As we engage with these technologies, we witness the blurring lines between human and machine communication, challenging traditional language proficiency and comprehension notions.

The educational landscape has also experienced a paradigm shift in integrating AI and language. Intelligent tutoring systems leverage AI to personalize learning experiences, adapting to individual needs and pacing. Artificial intelligence (AI)-driven language learning apps provide dynamic, immersive settings that mimic real-world conversational situations, improving language learning. Moreover, AI algorithms analyze vast amounts of linguistic data to identify trends and patterns, informing educators about effective teaching strategies and curriculum development. This symbiotic relationship between language and AI revolutionizes the learning process and opens new avenues for education accessibility and inclusivity.

How AI-driven language technologies are incorporated into our daily lives has completely changed the concept of personal help. Virtual assistants, who can comprehend and react to natural language commands, have become commonplace companions. Examples of these assistants are Siri, Alexa, and Google Assistant.These AI entities execute tasks and anticipate user needs through continuous learning and adaptation. The amalgamation of language and AI in personal assistance has streamlined daily activities, from setting reminders and sending messages to controlling smart home devices. However, this convenience raises questions about privacy, data security, and the ethical implications of entrusting AI systems with intimate aspects of our lives.

It is crucial to consider ethical issues when integrating language and AI. The growing impact of AI systems on decision-making procedures raises concerns about accountability, transparency, and bias. Language models trained on vast datasets may perpetuate existing biases present in the data, leading to discriminatory outcomes. Ensuring fairness and equity in AI-driven language applications requires a concerted effort to address these biases and establish ethical guidelines for development and deployment. Additionally, the transparency of AI algorithms and the accountability of the organizations behind them are crucial for building trust in these systems. Striking a balance between technological advancement and ethical responsibility is imperative to harness the full potential of language and AI integration.

The cultural and societal implications of language and AI integration are profound, influencing how we communicate and shaping our perceptions and understanding of the world. The rise of deepfake technology, which uses AI-generated content to manipulate audio and video, challenges the authenticity of language and media. This calls for increased awareness and critical literacy skills to navigate the digital landscape responsibly. Moreover, the globalization facilitated by AI language translation services has the potential to preserve and promote linguistic diversity while also homogenizing language use. Striking a balance between the advantages of global connectivity and preserving cultural and linguistic heritage becomes a delicate task in this context.

Chapter VI

Cultural Preservation
in the Digital Age

Digital Initiatives for Language Revitalization

Language faces unprecedented challenges in the digital age as a carrier of cultural identity and heritage. Globalization, urbanization, and the dominance of major world languages threaten the survival of many indigenous and minority languages. Notwithstanding these obstacles, digital projects have become effective instruments for language revitalization. This section investigates the role of digital efforts in language revitalization, looking at how technology can be used to protect, promote, and revive endangered languages.

Digital language revitalization programs cover a wide range of tactics and resources, each specifically designed to address a particular community's linguistic and cultural peculiarities. One of the critical approaches involves the development of language learning applications and online platforms. These digital tools leverage interactive and immersive experiences to engage learners in language acquisition. Mobile applications like Duolingo and Memrise offer gamified language learning experiences that make the process enjoyable and accessible to a broad audience. Similarly, online platforms like Rosetta stone and Transparent Language provide comprehensive language courses incorporating multimedia elements to enhance the learning experience. By making language learning available at users' fingertips, these initiatives break down geographical barriers and reach individuals beyond the immediate community, fostering a global network of language learners.

Additionally, social media platforms have been essential to language revitalization initiatives. Communities, organizations, and individuals dedicated to preserving endangered languages utilize platforms like Facebook, Twitter, and Instagram to share language resources, host virtual events, and connect with like-minded enthusiasts. The interactive nature of social media allows for real-time communication and collaboration, creating a dynamic space for language revitalization discussions. Hashtags like #LanguageRevitalization and #SpeakYourLanguage act as unifying symbols, uniting individuals with varying linguistic backgrounds towards conserving and advancing linguistic variety. Thus, social media serves as a virtual agora where language activists, teachers, and speakers share information, resources, and encouragement.

Through the creation of immersive language experiences, augmented reality (AR) and virtual reality (VR) technology present novel approaches to language revitalization. AR applications can overlay digital information, such as translations or cultural context, onto the physical world through smartphones or AR glasses. For example, a user exploring a museum exhibit can use AR to receive information about artifacts in their indigenous language, thereby connecting linguistic knowledge with cultural heritage. Conversely, virtual reality (VR) allows people to live in virtual worlds where they can interact with situations that call for language use. Language learners can practice conversations, navigate virtual communities, and participate in cultural rituals, all within a digital realm that facilitates language acquisition. These technologies bridge the gap between traditional language learning methods and contemporary digital experiences, providing a holistic approach to language revitalization.

Crowdsourcing and community-driven initiatives form another vital aspect of digital language revitalization. Platforms like the Living Tongues Institute's "Talking Dictionaries" and the Endangered Languages Project empower communities to document and share their languages. By utilizing community members' combined knowledge and experience, these efforts build extensive online linguistic resource repositories that include dictionaries, audio recordings, and grammar instructions. Through community participation in the documentation process, these digital efforts support language preservation while also enabling speakers to take an active role in the resuscitation of their native tongue. Moreover, the collaborative nature of crowdsourcing fosters a sense of collective responsibility and shared ownership of language revitalization efforts.

A potent new media for the transmission and preservation of oral histories, folktales, and cultural narratives in endangered languages is digital storytelling. Communities can produce and disseminate multimedia content that captures the diversity of their linguistic and cultural history through podcasts, YouTube channels, and digital archives. Beyond written documentation, digital storytelling captures the subtleties of tone, pronunciation, and emotion inherent in spoken communication. Projects such as the Global Recordings Network establish a digital repository of stories, songs, and conversations in endangered languages through audio-visual assets. This contributes to the generational transfer of cultural knowledge and is a valuable tool for language learners.

Machine translation and natural language processing technologies offer unique opportunities for language revitalization by automating the translation of digital content into endangered languages. Online articles, educational materials, and digital resources can be translated and made accessible to speakers of endangered languages, breaking down the language barrier in the digital realm. However, using machine translation in language revitalization raises ethical considerations, as the technology may only partially capture the cultural nuances and context embedded in the language. Striking a balance between the efficiency of machine translation and the preservation of linguistic and cultural authenticity is a challenge that requires careful consideration in developing and deploying these technologies.

Despite the entire advantages internet projects offer for language revitalization, problems exist. Access to technology remains a barrier, particularly in marginalized and remote communities. The digital gap makes already-existing disparities worse by making it more difficult for some groups to participate in language revival initiatives. Moreover, the rapid evolution of technology necessitates ongoing adaptation and upskilling, posing challenges for communities with limited resources. Additionally, the risk of digital content overshadowing traditional oral and community-based learning methods raises concerns about the potential loss of embodied linguistic knowledge passed down through generations. Striking a balance between technological innovation and the preservation of traditional modes of language transmission is crucial for the long-term sustainability of language revitalization efforts.

Impact of Digital Platforms on Minority Languages

The impact of digital platforms on language dynamics, especially those of minority languages, is significant and multifaceted in the era of digital globalization. Digital platforms, from social media and streaming services to online content creation, have become pervasive channels for communication, information dissemination, and cultural expression. While these platforms offer opportunities for minority languages to thrive in the digital realm, they also present challenges that can either bolster or erode linguistic diversity. The article explores the multifaceted impact of digital platforms on minority languages, examining how these technologies both empower and endanger linguistic richness, identity, and heritage.

Digital platforms, especially social media, have emerged as dynamic spaces where speakers of minority languages can connect, share, and celebrate their linguistic and cultural identities. Platforms like Facebook, Twitter, and Instagram provide a global stage for users to express themselves in their native languages, fostering a sense of community and solidarity among speakers of minority languages. Hashtags and online movements, often initiated by language activists and enthusiasts, serve as rallying points to promote linguistic diversity. Through social media, minority language speakers can share stories, anecdotes, and linguistic nuances, creating a digital tapestry that reflects the richness of their cultural and linguistic heritage. This interconnectedness strengthens the bonds between language groups and gives them a more significant global voice.

A democratizing force for linguistic expression, online content production enables speakers of minority languages to create and distribute information representing their viewpoints. Platforms like YouTube, TikTok, and podcast hosting services would allow individuals to create and share videos, music, and spoken-word content in their native languages. Speakers of minority languages now have more influence over narratives, may dispel misconceptions, and add to the global cultural landscape thanks to the democratization of content creation. For example, indigenous filmmakers can use YouTube to showcase their films, musicians can reach a global audience through digital platforms, and storytellers can share narratives that might otherwise remain confined to local communities. This ability to create and disseminate content in minority languages has the potential to counteract the dominance of major languages in mainstream media.

Digital platforms are also essential for the documentation and preservation of languages. The internet is a vast repository for linguistic resources, where minority language communities can archive dictionaries, grammatical guides, and audio-visual materials. Initiatives like the Endangered Languages Project and Living Tongues Institute leverage digital platforms to crowdsource linguistic data and create comprehensive online databases. Along with helping to preserve endangered languages, this digital documentation makes it easier for linguists, scholars, and community members to collaborate. Thanks to the digital archive, future generations will have access to a treasure of linguistic knowledge that might otherwise be lost to assimilation and time.

However, the impact of digital platforms on minority languages is not uniformly positive. The dominance of major speeches on the internet poses a significant challenge to the visibility and viability of minority languages in the digital space. Search engine algorithms, social media algorithms, and content moderation policies are often designed with major languages in mind, leading to the marginalization of content in minority languages. This digital marginalization reinforces existing power imbalances and limits the discoverability of minority language content. As a result, speakers of minority languages may find their digital presence constrained, hindering their ability to participate fully in the global digital discourse.

Additionally, the loss of linguistic diversity may result from English being the dominant language on the internet. Because English is the most widely used language online, speakers of minority languages may feel pressured to adopt it to become more visible and interact with users. This linguistic assimilation can lead to a gradual decline in the use and transmission of minority languages as speakers opt for the convenience of a widely understood global language. The digital divide exacerbates this issue, as communities with limited access to the internet may face challenges in preserving and promoting their tongues in the digital era.

There are further issues with language uniformity and authenticity brought forth by digital media. Speakers of minority languages may alter their linguistic expressions to conform to digital communication norms to increase online exposure and participation. This process of language adaptation for digital spaces can lead to the standardization of specific linguistic features, potentially eroding the authenticity and diversity of the language. The tension between linguistic preservation and adaptation for digital communication underscores the need for thoughtful language policies and community-led initiatives that balance the demands of the digital age with the integrity of minority languages.

In addition to linguistic considerations, digital platforms raise ethical questions about cultural appropriation and exploitation. As minority languages gain visibility online, there is a risk of their cultural elements being commodified and appropriated for commercial gain. Using indigenous languages in branding, marketing, and digital content creation without proper cultural context and consent can lead to the exploitation of linguistic and cultural heritage. Balancing the celebration and promotion of minority languages on digital platforms with the need to protect against cultural appropriation is a delicate task that requires collaboration between content creators, platform administrators, and linguistic communities.

The impact of digital platforms on minority languages extends beyond linguistic domains, influencing broader societal attitudes and perceptions. Representation and portrayal of minority languages in digital spaces can shape public perceptions and contribute to the preservation or erasure of linguistic diversity. A positive picture can foster pride and a sense of belonging among speakers of minority languages, while negative or stereotypical portrayals can reinforce biases and contribute to language stigmatization. Hence, to shape narratives representing the authenticity, diversity, and importance of minority languages in the digital sphere, content producers, digital platforms, and legislators play crucial roles.

Navigating Challenges to Preserve Linguistic Heritage

Language faces various challenges in the contemporary global landscape as a vessel of cultural identity and heritage. The interconnectedness brought about by globalization, coupled with the dominance of major languages in various spheres, poses a threat to the survival of linguistic diversity. Preserving linguistic heritage is a multifaceted task that involves navigating technological, social, economic, and educational challenges. The article explores the complex terrain of linguistic preservation, examining the challenges communities face and the strategies employed to safeguard their linguistic heritage.

While they provide never-before-seen possibilities for communication and knowledge exchange, technological innovations have positive and negative effects on language preservation. Positively, digital technology offers venues for the preservation, propagation, and resuscitation of endangered languages. Initiatives like the Endangered Languages Project and digital archives facilitate the creation of online repositories that house linguistic resources such as dictionaries, grammatical guides, and audio-visual materials. However, the same digital environment can present difficulties, especially regarding language standards and the predominance of significant languages in online contexts. The pressure to conform to the linguistic norms of major languages for broader online visibility may inadvertently contribute to the erosion of linguistic diversity, necessitating a delicate balance between digital integration and the preservation of authentic linguistic expressions.

Globalization, driven by economic and social forces, has led to increased mobility and intercultural exchanges, influencing language dynamics on a global scale. Although this connectivity promotes understanding between cultures, it also plays a role in linguistic assimilation. Since they are often limited to specific geographic regions, indigenous and minority languages run the risk of being supplanted by dominant languages. Economic factors, such as the pursuit of employment opportunities and educational prospects, can drive individuals and communities to adopt significant speeches at the expense of their native tongues. The economic imperative to communicate in languages that offer economic advantages in a globalized world poses a formidable challenge to preserving linguistic heritage. Addressing this challenge requires economic opportunities that value linguistic diversity and policies that recognize and support the importance of multilingualism.

Educational systems, pivotal in shaping linguistic attitudes and behaviors, play a central role in nurturing or undermining linguistic diversity. The dominance of major languages in formal education often marginalizes indigenous and minority languages. The standardization of curricula and the imposition of significant languages as mediums of instruction contribute to neglecting local languages in educational settings. Consequently, younger generations may grow up with limited proficiency in their ancestral languages, further exacerbating the threat to linguistic heritage. To counter this trend, there is a need for inclusive language policies in education that recognize the value of diverse linguistic repertoires. When used with dominant languages, bilingual and multilingual education models can effectively preserve linguistic history while guaranteeing students' access to a broader range of educational options.

As a potent tool for cultural transmission, the media is vital in forming language narratives and perspectives. However, the media landscape often reflects and perpetuates linguistic hierarchies, favoring major languages in news reporting, entertainment, and advertising. This linguistic bias contributes to the marginalization of minority languages and reinforces the perception that linguistic value is synonymous with the prevalence of a language in public discourse. Policies supporting minority languages in journalism, broadcasting, and digital media are needed to address this issue. Furthermore, encouraging a favorable representation of linguistic variety in the media might help shift public perceptions about lesser-spoken languages.

The problem of language endangerment, which occurs when social, economic, and environmental variables interact to hasten the extinction of particular languages, is another effect of globalization.

Indigenous communities, often residing in areas rich in biodiversity, face the dual challenge of environmental degradation and the erosion of their linguistic heritage. Ecological changes, driven by climate change and unsustainable practices, can disrupt traditional lifestyles and lead to the displacement of communities. This displacement and the economic pressures to assimilate into mainstream societies contribute to language loss. Therefore, efforts to preserve linguistic heritage must be accompanied by environmental conservation initiatives and sustainable development practices that respect the interconnectedness of languages, cultures, and ecosystems.

As a proactive response to language loss, language revitalization entails concerted attempts to reclaim, revitalize, and transfer linguistic knowledge to future generations. However, intergenerational transmission, shifting cultural settings, and the requirement for flexible teaching strategies provide obstacles for rehabilitation projects. In many cases, the elders who possess linguistic knowledge may face challenges in passing it on to younger generations who are more influenced by dominant languages and globalized cultural trends. Additionally, the context in which languages are spoken continuously evolves, requiring revitalization efforts to be dynamic and responsive to changing social, economic, and technological landscapes.

Preserving linguistic heritage is not solely the responsibility of linguistic communities; it requires the active involvement of governments, policymakers, and international organizations. Language policies at the national and international levels play a pivotal role in supporting or undermining linguistic diversity.

Recognition of linguistic rights, developing inclusive language policies, and implementing measures to support minority languages are essential components of a comprehensive strategy for linguistic preservation. Through campaigns like the Organization for Education, Science, and Culture of the United Nations (UNESCO) has adopted a major contribution to linguistic diversity with the International Year of Indigenous Languages, an initiative to increase awareness of the critical global condition of indigenous languages.

Furthermore, collaborations between linguistic communities and academic institutions can yield valuable insights and resources for linguistic preservation. Linguists and scholars are indispensable when preserving endangered languages, producing linguistic materials, and formulating plans for language preservation. Collaborative projects involving community members in the documentation process, such as the Living Tongues Institute's "Talking Dictionaries," contribute to the empowerment of linguistic communities in preserving their heritage.

Chapter VII

Language Learning in the Digital Era

Digital Platforms Transforming Language Education

The education landscape is profoundly transformed in the digital era, and language learning is at the forefront of this revolution. Digital platforms have become powerful tools for reshaping how languages are taught and learned, breaking down barriers of time and space, and providing learners with unprecedented access to diverse linguistic resources. The section explores the impact of digital platforms on language education, delving into how technology is reshaping teaching methodologies, expanding learning opportunities, and fostering a more interconnected and dynamic language learning environment.

Digital platforms have revolutionized language education by providing learners with interactive and immersive experiences beyond traditional classroom settings. Applications for learning languages, including Duolingo, Rosetta Stone, and Babbel, use gamification strategies to make learning fun and engaging. These platforms offer a range of exercises, quizzes, and challenges that cater to different learning styles, making language acquisition more personalized and accessible. Additionally, because these programs are portable, students can practice whenever and wherever they choose, turning downtime into beneficial opportunities for language reinforcement. Integrating artificial intelligence (AI) in these platforms enhances adaptability, as the algorithms can tailor the learning experience to individual progress, addressing specific strengths and weaknesses.

Global connectedness is another benefit of online language learning platforms, which let students communicate with language lovers and native speakers worldwide. Tandem and HelloTalk are two examples of language exchange services that pair users with native speakers so they can improve their language skills via text, phone, or video chat. This fosters authentic language use, cultural exchange, and the development of conversational skills. Additionally, digital platforms enable collaborative learning through virtual classrooms, where students and instructors from diverse locations can unite. Platforms like Zoom, Google Meet, and Microsoft Teams have become essential tools for synchronous language learning, providing real-time interaction, collaboration, and feedback, thus breaking down geographical barriers and creating a global community of language learners.

Since Massive Open Online Courses (MOOCs) were introduced, language instruction has changed even more. Students now have access to top-notch courses from esteemed universities worldwide. Resources such as Coursera, edX, and FutureLearn provide a wide range of language classes delivered by qualified teachers. These courses are designed to meet students' varied requirements and interests by offering a broad choice of language partners, specialty themes, and ability levels. Because MOOCs are flexible, students can interact with the material at their own speed, increasing accessibility to language instruction and considering a range of schedules and obligations. Additionally, the availability of MOOCs encourages lifetime learning by allowing people to continue their language studies after conventional school deadlines have passed.

Digital platforms have also transformed the process of evaluating and certifying languages. These exams frequently have adaptive elements that use artificial intelligence (AI) to adjust the test's difficulty according to the test-taker's performance, giving a more accurate language proficiency assessment. The shift towards digital assessments enhances efficiency, reduces administrative barriers, and enables quick and secure test delivery. This digital transformation in language assessment contributes to the recognition and standardization of language proficiency, which is essential in academic, professional, and immigration contexts.

Furthermore, the rise of language learning platforms integrating technologies related to augmented reality (AR) and virtual reality (VR) redefines language education by providing immersive and realistic experiences. AR applications overlay digital information onto the physical world, allowing learners to engage with language content in real-world contexts. For example, language learners can use AR apps to identify and label objects in their environment with their corresponding names in the target language, enhancing vocabulary acquisition and contextual understanding. On the other hand, VR technologies create simulated environments where learners can interact with native speakers, participate in virtual scenarios, and practice language skills in a dynamic and lifelike setting. This level of immersion goes beyond traditional language learning methods, offering a more holistic and experiential approach to language acquisition.

Digital platforms are revolutionizing language instruction and making it more accessible to a broader range of learners. Language education has come to rely heavily on Open Educational Resources (OERs), freely available digital assets for instruction, learning, and research. Platforms like OpenStax, MIT OpenCourseWare, and Khan Academy provide educators and learners with many language resources, including textbooks, multimedia content, and interactive exercises. This open-access model reduces financial barriers to education, making high-quality language learning materials available to a global audience. Additionally, collaborative platforms like Wikipedia and Wikibooks enable the creation and sharing of language-related content by educators, linguists, and enthusiasts, fostering a culture of knowledge exchange and collaboration in the digital space.

However, there are drawbacks to the digital revolution in language learning. One significant concern is the potential for the digital divide to widen existing educational inequalities. Access to technology, high-speed internet, and digital devices varies widely across regions and socioeconomic groups. Learners in underserved communities may face barriers to online language education, limiting their language acquisition opportunities. In order to close the digital divide, coordinated efforts by efforts by policymakers, educators, and technology providers to ensure equitable access to digital platforms and resources for all learners.

Moreover, the reliance on digital platforms raises questions about data privacy and security. Language learning applications and online platforms often collect vast amounts of data on learner behavior, preferences, and performance. Safeguarding this sensitive information is paramount to protecting learners' privacy, especially considering the increasing integration of AI in language education. Ethical considerations surrounding data collection, storage, and usage must be addressed to build trust and ensure the responsible use of learner data in the digital language learning ecosystem.

The function of teachers in the digital age is evolving, requiring a shift towards a more facilitative and adaptive teaching approach. Even if digital platforms provide many interactive tools and materials, human interaction is still essential in language learning. Effective technology integration in language teaching requires educators to become proficient in digital devices, adapt their pedagogical approaches, and guide learners in navigating the digital landscape. Professional development opportunities that focus on digital literacy, technology integration, and innovative teaching methodologies are essential to empower educators to harness the full potential of digital platforms in language education.

Challenges and Opportunities in Online Language Learning

Online language learning has become a potent and adaptable method in the ever-changing field of education, allowing students to pick up new languages at a distance. This digital shift has brought about many challenges and opportunities, shaping how languages are taught and learned. The section explores the multifaceted landscape of online language learning, delving into the challenges that learners and educators face while highlighting the transformative opportunities that digital platforms present for language acquisition.

One of the primary challenges in online language learning is the digital divide, exacerbating existing educational inequalities. While the internet has become an essential tool for accessing language courses and resources, not all learners have equal access to digital devices and high-speed internet. Learners in underserved communities, both in developed and developing regions may face barriers to participating in online language courses, limiting their opportunities for language acquisition. The digital divide must be closed, but it will take coordinated efforts from legislators, educators, and technology providers to ensure that online language learning is accessible to learners across diverse socioeconomic backgrounds.

One additional area for improvement associated with online language learning is the possibility of less in-person interaction. Traditional language classrooms provide a setting for real-time communication, immediate feedback, and social interaction among learners. In contrast, online language courses, particularly self-paced ones, may lack the interpersonal dynamics contributing to language development. Lack of in-person interaction can impede the growth of spoken language abilities and cultural competency. Educators must navigate this challenge by integrating synchronous elements into online courses, such as virtual classrooms, video conferencing, and language exchange opportunities, to facilitate real-time interaction and interpersonal communication.

Security and privacy of data are important issues in the online language learning environment. Many language learning platforms collect extensive data on learner behavior, preferences, and performance to tailor the learning experience. Protecting this sensitive information is essential to ensure the privacy and security of learners. Ethical data collection, storage, and utilization issues need to be considered to foster trust and protect learner privacy in the digital language learning ecosystem. Robust regulations and guidelines governing the ethical use of learner data in online language learning platforms must be established by legislators and technology companies.

While challenges exist, online language learning also presents transformative opportunities that enhance the efficiency and effectiveness of language acquisition. The flexibility and accessibility provided by digital channels represent one significant possibility. Online language courses allow learners to engage with language materials at their own pace, breaking down the constraints of traditional classroom schedules. Working professionals notably benefit from this flexibility. Students with varied commitments, and individuals with diverse learning styles. Access to language resources anytime and anywhere empowers learners to tailor their language learning experience to their needs and preferences.

Moreover, combining technology, encompassing artificial intelligence (AI) and machine learning provides tailored educational opportunities in virtual language programs. Adaptive learning algorithms can analyze learner performance, identify strengths and shortcomings, and modify the text to address individual learning needs. Language learning applications like Duolingo and Babbel leverage AI to provide targeted exercises, vocabulary suggestions, and adaptive quizzes, creating a personalized and dynamic learning environment. This tailored method meets language learners' various needs and skill levels while improving student engagement.

The global connectivity facilitated by online language learning platforms presents another significant opportunity. Learners can connect with language speakers and enthusiasts worldwide, creating an international community of language learners. Language exchange platforms, social media groups, and virtual classrooms enable learners to practice their target language with native speakers, fostering authentic language use and cultural exchange. This interconnectedness contributes to a more immersive language learning experience, allowing learners to engage with diverse accents, dialects, and cultural contexts.

Being able to access a wide range of digital resources that enhance language learning is another benefit of online language instruction. Open Educational Resources (OERs), digital textbooks, multimedia content, and language exchange websites provide learners with many resources beyond traditional books. These resources enhance the diversity of learning materials, offering a range of content tailored to different learning styles and preferences. Learners can access authentic materials such as movies, podcasts, and news articles, immersing themselves in the language and culture they are learning.

The abundance of digital resources supports language acquisition and fosters a culture of lifelong learning and exploration.

Moreover, the gamification of online language learning platforms introduces an element of play and competition that motivates learners. Language learning applications often incorporate gamified elements, such as points, levels, and rewards, to engage learners in language acquisition. This gamified approach makes language learning enjoyable, motivating learners to progress and achieve milestones. The competitive aspects, such as leaderboards and challenges, create a sense of community and camaraderie among learners, fostering a positive and collaborative learning environment.

Literacy and Knowledge Dissemination in a Digital Landscape

Literacy has taken on new dimensions in the fast-evolving digital landscape, transforming how information is accessed, disseminated, and consumed. The emergence of digital technology has changed conventional ideas of literacy, extending its reach beyond simple reading and writing comprehension to include a multifaceted range of competencies necessary for maneuvering through the enormous and ever-changing ocean of digital data. The intricate relationship between literacy and knowledge transmission in the digital age is explored in this article, along with the opportunities and problems that present themselves as we traverse this quickly evolving information landscape.

Digital literacy, in its contemporary sense, goes beyond the ability to read and write; it encompasses the skills required to engage with, evaluate, and create digital content critically. With the rise of the internet and the proliferation of digital platforms, individuals need to be adept at navigating a diverse range of digital media, understanding information sources, and discerning the credibility of online content.

In a time when false information may travel quickly, swaying public opinion and forming narratives, the capacity to assess knowledge critically is essential. Therefore, digital literacy is vital to equipping people to be knowledgeable and discriminating information consumers in the digital world.

An important issue facing the digital age is the overabundance of information. The abundance of digital content available at our fingertips can be overwhelming, making it challenging for individuals to filter through the noise and find reliable, relevant information. Consequently, digital literacy encompasses the capacity to retrieve data and the ability to select, evaluate, and combine it. Individuals must develop strategies to manage information overload, employing critical thinking and information literacy skills to sift through vast datasets and extract meaningful insights.

The democratization of information dissemination is a notable opportunity in the digital landscape. Digital platforms, mainly social media, have provided individuals unprecedented opportunities to share their ideas, perspectives, and expertise with a global audience. Blogs, podcasts, YouTube channels, and social media profiles have become powerful mediums for knowledge dissemination, allowing individuals to bypass traditional gatekeepers and directly connect with diverse audiences. This democratization of information empowers individuals to contribute to the global pool of knowledge, fostering a more inclusive and diverse discourse.

On the other hand, the problem of disinformation and the proliferation of fake news is the opposite of this democratization. The ease with which information can be disseminated on digital platforms, often without proper verification, poses a significant threat to data integrity. Misleading content, intentional misinformation campaigns and deep fakes can erode public trust and contribute to the spread of falsehoods. Navigating this landscape requires a heightened sense of media literacy, with individuals being equipped to critically evaluate the sources, motives, and context of online information.

The dynamics of literacy in the digital landscape also extend to issues of access and inclusivity. At the same time, the internet has provided unprecedented access to information, but a digital divide persists, creating disparities in access to technology and online resources. Socioeconomic factors, geographical location, and infrastructure limitations contribute to a digital range that hinders specific populations from fully participating in the digital discourse. Bridging this divide requires concerted efforts to ensure equitable access to digital tools, resources, and connectivity, fostering a more inclusive and diverse online community.

Multimodal literacy is another dimension that has gained prominence in the digital era. As communication becomes increasingly visual and interactive, individuals must be adept at interpreting and creating content across various modes, including text, images, videos, and interactive elements. Navigating and understanding multimedia content is crucial for effective communication and knowledge dissemination in the digital landscape. Additionally, individuals are increasingly engaging in content creation, producing multimedia materials to share information and perspectives. This shift towards multimodal literacy highlights the need for individuals to develop skills in visual literacy, digital storytelling, and multimedia production.

The digital landscape has also witnessed the rise of online education platforms, transforming how knowledge is disseminated and acquired. Learning management systems, educational material repositories, and Massive Open Online Courses (MOOCs) give students access to knowledge from professionals and institutions worldwide. Platforms for online learning are flexible, allowing people to pursue education on their own schedule and at their own speed. For those who encounter obstacles in their pursuit of traditional educational paths, in particular, this democratization of education represents a huge potential.

However, the legitimacy and caliber of online courses provide additional difficulties for online learning. Because there is so much online content, it can be difficult for students to distinguish between high-quality and low-quality online learning tools. Mechanisms for credentialing and accreditation are crucial for confirming the legitimacy and caliber of online learning programs. Additionally, the digital divide may limit access to online education for specific populations, reinforcing existing inequalities in educational opportunities.

The relationship between literacy and the spread of knowledge is further complicated by the development of artificial intelligence (AI) and machine learning. The information that people see on digital platforms is influenced by the curation and recommendation of content by artificial intelligence algorithms. The tailoring of material delivery by algorithms begs the subject of filter bubbles—the phenomenon in which people are exposed to information that confirms their preexisting opinions and preferences. Digital literacy requires knowing how artificial intelligence (AI) affects information consumption and being conscious of potential biases in algorithmic recommendations.

As significant participants in the digital sphere, social media platforms significantly influence public conversation and the diffusion of knowledge. These platforms serve as both information sources and arenas for public engagement, allowing individuals to share, discuss, and debate various topics. However, social media also amplifies echo chambers, where individuals are exposed to information that aligns with their beliefs, contributing to polarization and reinforcing ideological bubbles. Therefore, using social media effectively calls for higher media literacy, critical thinking, and the capacity to participate in thoughtful, productive conversations.

The phenomenon of "viral" information on social media is another example of how difficult it is to disseminate knowledge in the digital era. Whether accurate or not, news can spread rapidly through online networks, shaping public opinion and influencing narratives. The viral nature of content introduces challenges related to fact-checking, information verification, and the responsibility of individuals to assess the information they encounter and share critically. In this situation, media literacy becomes an essential ability that enables people to move around the digital world with judgment and critical awareness.

Chapter VIII

The Fusion of Language and Visual Elements

Memes: Cultural and Linguistic Phenomena in the Digital Space

In the digital age, where information is disseminated at unprecedented speeds through interconnected networks, memes have emerged as powerful and pervasive cultural artifacts. Originating as simple images with captions, memes have evolved into complex cultural and linguistic phenomena that transcend geographical and linguistic boundaries. This section explores the intricate nature of memes, delving into their origins, evolution, and their role as both cultural and linguistic expressions in the digital space.

Memes, in the context of internet culture, refer to images, videos, or text that are humorously altered and shared widely online. In "The Selfish Gene," published in 1976, Richard Dawkins first used the term "meme" to refer to ideas that propagate and change culturally. However, the contemporary understanding of memes has transformed into a digital phenomenon where humorous, relatable, or satirical content is rapidly disseminated across various online platforms.

The evolution of memes is closely tied to the dynamics of internet culture and the participatory nature of online communities. Early internet memes, such as the "Dancing Baby" or "Hamster Dance," were simple animations that gained popularity in the early days of the World Wide Web. As internet platforms diversified, the meme format adapted, incorporating image macros, reaction images, and exploitable templates. Memes' simplicity—often combined with relatability and humor—contributes to their virality and extensive distribution.

Memes are a mirror of modern culture; they capture humor, morals, and common experiences. They are a type of digital folklore that conveys cultural concepts in an understandable and succinct manner. Memes frequently make references to films, TV series, music, and other forms of popular culture, establishing a common vocabulary that appeals to a wide range of viewers. The cultural significance of memes lies in their ability to encapsulate societal trends, critique norms, and provide a sense of belonging to online communities.

Moreover, memes act as a means of cultural commentary and satire. Through the manipulation of images and text, memes can convey nuanced messages, critique societal issues, or offer a humorous take on current events. Memes' capacity to defy expectations, contrast disparate aspects, or offer astute insight on social problems is frequently what gives them their comedy. This humorous element is a potent technique for drawing viewers in and promoting cross-cultural communication.

Beyond their cultural significance, memes exhibit distinct linguistic features that contribute to their widespread appeal. Memes frequently incorporate wordplay, puns, and other forms of linguistic manipulation. The brevity and conciseness of meme captions necessitate a keen understanding of language nuances, allowing creators to convey humor or commentary within a limited space. Memes also play with linguistic conventions, subverting expectations and creating a unique form of online language.

The use of memes as a linguistic tool extends to the creation of internet-specific languages and expressions. Online forums gave rise to internet slang phrases like "LOL," "OMG," and "ROFL," which have since spread to other forms of digital communication. Memes contribute to the evolution of language by introducing new words, phrases, and linguistic conventions that become part of the digital lexicon. Memes spread quickly, which speeds up the adoption of these language improvements.

Memes' visual component is just as important to their ability to communicate. Memes often rely on semiotic elements, utilizing images, symbols, and visual metaphors to convey meaning. Memes employ visual semiotics, which entails manipulating identifiable pictures to establish a common visual language that amplifies the message's impact. The juxtaposition of images and text in memes adds layers of meaning and contributes to their humor and communicative efficiency.

Moreover, memes often engage with intertextuality, referencing and remixing familiar cultural symbols. Memes are able to draw on the viewer's preexisting cultural knowledge through intertextual play, which fosters a sense of understanding among members of online communities. The recycling and repurposing of visual elements contribute to the evolution of meme formats and the creation of meme templates that can be adapted to various contexts.

Memes are essential in forming an online community's identity. Communities on social media platforms, forums, and specialized websites create their own meme cultures, complete with inside jokes and specialized allusions that characterize the culture of the group. Memes become a form of digital vernacular, shaping the way members communicate, express solidarity, and differentiate themselves from broader online cultures.

Memes are frequently used in online communities to strengthen group cohesiveness and foster a sense of community among participants. Shared memes serve as cultural indicators, indicating insider information and conversation engagement within the community. Memes also serve as a form of online ritual, with certain memes becoming emblematic of specific online spaces and their unique subcultures.

Despite their ubiquity and cultural relevance, memes are not without challenges and controversies. One significant issue is the potential for memes to perpetuate stereotypes, reinforce biases, or contribute to the spread of misinformation. Memes based on gender, racial, or cultural stereotypes have the potential to reinforce negative narratives, underscoring the importance of critically evaluating meme content.

Additionally, the fast-paced and decentralized nature of meme creation can lead to the rapid spread of misinformation. Memes frequently oversimplify complicated subjects, and the lighthearted setting can make it difficult to distinguish between facts and satire. This prompts questions about how memes might affect public conversation and how media literacy is necessary to understand the subtleties of internet content.

The use of images and content in memes raises legal and ethical questions regarding copyright and ownership. Memes often repurpose copyrighted material, leading to debates about the boundaries of fair use and intellectual property. Memes' tendency to become viral can occasionally lead to the unattributed usage of original content, which raises questions regarding content authors' rights.

While some argue that memes fall under fair use as transformative works, others contend that the widespread sharing and modification of memes can have economic implications for content creators. Striking a balance between the creative expression enabled by memes and the protection of intellectual property rights remains an ongoing challenge in the digital landscape.

Memes have also become prominent tools in political discourse, serving as a means of expression, criticism, and mobilization. Political memes leverage humor, satire, and visual semiotics to convey political messages, critique public figures, or engage with current events. The share ability and virality of memes make them effective tools for political communication, reaching a wide audience and shaping public perceptions.

Memes in politics are not without controversy, though. Political memes can contribute to the polarization of online spaces, reinforce echo chambers, and simplify complex political issues. The potential for memes to oversimplify or distort information raises questions about their impact on public understanding and civic discourse.

Visual Language: Beyond Words

In the rich tapestry of human communication, words have long held a central role, serving as the primary vehicle for expressing thoughts, ideas, and emotions. However, a vibrant and nuanced realm of communication exists alongside the written and spoken word—visual language. Visual language extends beyond the confines of written and spoken communication, encompassing various symbols, images, and gestures that convey meaning. This section explores the multifaceted nature of visual language, examining its historical roots, cultural significance, and ever-expanding role in the contemporary digital landscape.

Using visual symbols to convey meaning predates written language, with ancient civilizations relying on pictograms and ideograms to communicate ideas. The Sumerians, Egyptians, and Mayans, among others, employed visual symbols carved into stone or written on papyrus to record information, tell stories, and communicate across language barriers. These early forms of visual language laid the groundwork for the evolution of written scripts and highlighted the innate human inclination to communicate through optical means.

The advent of written language did not diminish the importance of visual symbols; instead, it introduced a dynamic interplay between written and visual modes of communication. Manuscripts and illuminated texts from medieval times adorned with intricate illustrations served as repositories of written knowledge and visual narratives that enriched the reader's understanding. The blend of text and image in religious texts, such as illuminated manuscripts, conveyed complex theological concepts to a largely illiterate audience, emphasizing the symbiotic relationship between words and visuals.

Visual language transcends linguistic and cultural barriers, offering a universal mode of communication that resonates with diverse audiences. Religious icons, flags of nations, and traditional artwork are examples of cultural symbols that act as potent visual communicators, capturing intricate cultural narratives and identities. Visual language enables the transmission of cultural heritage, allowing societies to pass down stories, traditions, and values visually, often with a potency that words alone may struggle to convey.

Additionally, visual language is crucial in forming identity and communal memory. Historical events are often memorialized through visual representations, such as paintings, sculptures, and photographs. In addition to serving as historical records, these visual artifacts help shape national narratives and collective identities.

Using images in storytelling changes history by evoking emotions and forming memories in ways that words alone cannot.

In advertising and marketing, visual language is harnessed to evoke emotions, convey messages, and create brand identities. Logos, color schemes, and pictorial motifs become synonymous with particular brands, establishing a visual vocabulary consumers recognize and associate with specific products or services. Visual language in advertising is powerful because it can quickly convey ideas and elicit a visceral reaction, sometimes obviating the need for lengthy textual explanations.

Nonverbal communication, a significant component of visual language, encompasses gestures, facial expressions, body language, and other visual cues that convey meaning without relying on words. The universality of specific nonverbal cues allows for cross-cultural communication, as terms like smiles, frowns, and hand gestures can transcend linguistic differences. In interpersonal communication, nonverbal cues often carry emotional nuances and provide context that complements or contradicts verbal messages.

Visual language also includes sign language, which is a highly developed gesture communication method used by the Deaf community. American Sign Language (ASL) and other sign languages worldwide employ a rich vocabulary of hand shapes, movements, and facial expressions to convey complex thoughts and emotions. Sign languages demonstrate the adaptability and expressiveness of visual forms of communication, challenging the idea that language is intrinsically linked to spoken or written words.

In the digital age, the significance of visual language has reached new heights, driven by the proliferation of visual content on digital platforms. Specifically on social media, images, videos, and emojis have taken center stage in communication, creating a visually-centric environment. Visual storytelling is given priority on platforms like Instagram, Snapchat, and TikTok, which let users express stories, feelings, and experiences via well-chosen images.

Memes, a standard online visual communication format, are a prime example of the dynamic interaction between text and pictures. Memes use text, images, and cultural allusions to express comedy, commentary, and shared experiences. Memes become viral because they can condense complicated concepts into short, approachable graphics, which helps online groups feel more connected and culturally aware of one another.

The rise of infographics and data visualization further underscores the importance of visual language in the digital landscape. Complex information and statistics are transformed into visually engaging graphics, making data more accessible and understandable to a broad audience. Infographics are used as lobbying, teaching, and narrative techniques in various fields, including academics and journalism, as well as practical communication tools.

Digital storytelling, facilitated by multimedia elements, has become a prominent mode of expression. Platforms like YouTube and podcasting integrate visual and auditory components to create immersive narratives. Visual elements, whether in video footage, animations, or graphics, enhance the storytelling experience, engaging audiences in ways that traditional written or spoken narratives alone might not achieve.

Visual language has many advantages for communication, but it also has drawbacks and subtleties. The potential for misinterpretation exists when graphic symbols carry different cultural or contextual meanings. Images that appear to be understood by everyone may have culturally distinct meanings, necessitating careful consideration of the target audience.

Visual manipulation, facilitated by photo editing software, raises concerns about the authenticity and trustworthiness of visual content. The prevalence of edited images on social media platforms challenges the integrity of online visual communication, prompting discussions about the ethical use of digital manipulation tools and the need for media literacy.

Another factor to take into account while discussing visual language is accessibility. While visual content can be engaging and impactful, it may pose challenges for individuals with visual impairments or disabilities. The accessibility improvement initiatives include employing audio explanations, offering alternate text descriptions for images, and ensuring that text-based information accompanies visual content.

Challenges and Nuances of Visual Communication

Visual communication, conveying information and ideas through visual elements, has become integral to our daily lives; in a time of digital media and Rapid technological advancements, the significance of visual communication cannot be overstated. But as we move through this visually-driven environment, we come across various obstacles and subtleties that influence the potency and impact of visual communications.

One prominent challenge lies in the diverse ways individuals interpret visual stimuli. Cultural differences, background experiences, and personal perspectives significantly influence how people perceive images. What may be a universally understood symbol in one culture might carry entirely different connotations in another. This cultural nuance underscores the importance of considering the audience when crafting visual messages to ensure they resonate positively and avoid unintended misinterpretations.

Moreover, the swift advancement of technology poses obstacles to the adjustment and application of novel visual communication instruments. As cutting-edge innovations in augmented and virtual reality become more prevalent, communicators must grapple with the complexities of integrating these tools into their strategies. The learning curve associated with mastering these technologies and understanding their potential applications adds a layer of difficulty, especially for individuals and organizations with limited resources.

Social media's emergence as the primary medium for visual communication amplifies the challenge of maintaining authenticity and credibility. In a world inundated with visuals vying for attention, the temptation to prioritize sensationalism over substance is ever-present. This compromises the validity of information conveyed visually and lessens the efficacy of visual communication. Striking the right balance between engaging content and accurate representation becomes a delicate task in this environment.

Another critical component of visual communication that requires consideration is accessibility. Although images can be effective tools for communicating ideas, they may inadvertently exclude individuals with visual impairments. This raises ethical concerns, prompting communicators to explore inclusive design principles to ensure their visual messages are accessible to diverse audiences. Incorporating alternative text, using high-contrast colors, and providing audio descriptions are essential to fostering inclusivity in visual communication.

The pervasive nature of visual content in the digital age also brings forth concerns related to privacy and consent. As individuals share and consume vast amounts of visual information online, the lines between public and private spaces blur. Striking a balance between the desire for visual storytelling and respecting individuals' right to privacy becomes increasingly challenging. Navigating these ethical considerations is crucial to maintaining trust and integrity in visual communication.

In addition to these challenges, the sheer volume of visual stimuli bombarding individuals daily contributes to information overload. Communicators need to use tactics that capture their audience's attention rapidly because people's attention spans are getting shorter when they are constantly exposed to pictures. One must create concise, powerful, and aesthetically appealing messaging to break through the clutter and make an impression.

Moreover, the evolving nature of visual trends poses a constant challenge for communicators aiming to stay relevant. What is practical and aesthetically pleasing now might need to be updated or more balanced tomorrow. It takes a great awareness of current visual trends and the flexibility to adjust techniques to navigate this changing world. Keeping abreast of these trends risks rendering visible communication efforts obsolete and ineffective.

For example, the psychological effects of images significantly influence how people interpret and react to information. Colors, shapes, and images can evoke emotions and influence decision-making, making it imperative for communicators to harness the psychological nuances of visuals to achieve specific objectives.

Moreover, it is impossible to overstate the significance of context in visual communication. The same visible message may carry vastly different meanings depending on the context in which it is presented. Communicators can adapt graphics to particular situations by knowing the complexities of context, which guarantees that the intended message conforms to the prevailing circumstances and cultural standards.

Effective visual communication also requires a keen awareness of the power dynamics. The people saw how the images are put together, and the photos themselves can either support or undermine the power structures in place. Understanding how images can reinforce stereotypes or provide voice to underrepresented groups emphasizes communicators' duty to use images sensibly and morally.

Chapter IX

Cybersecurity
and Language Heritage

Securing Linguistic Interactions in the Digital Realm

In an age dominated by digital connectivity, linguistic interactions have transcended traditional boundaries, paving the way for unprecedented communication possibilities. As the digital realm becomes increasingly integral to our daily lives, the need for securing linguistic interactions has emerged as a critical concern. This section explores the multifaceted dimensions of securing linguistic interactions in the digital sphere, delving into the challenges posed by cyber threats, the importance of encryption, the role of artificial intelligence in language security, and the ethical considerations accompanying the quest for digital communication safety.

In the digital age, cyber security is critical to protecting language exchanges. With the proliferation of online communication channels, the vulnerability of linguistic data to cyber threats has escalated. Hackers, identity thieves, and malicious actors exploit weaknesses in digital infrastructure to gain unauthorized access to linguistic interactions, posing threats to individuals, organizations, and even nations. The imperative to safeguard linguistic data from cyber attacks has led to the development of robust cyber security measures, ranging from firewalls and secure sockets layer (SSL) protocols to advanced intrusion detection systems. Since the digital environment is constantly changing, maintaining adequate language security demands ongoing attention to detail and flexibility in response to new and emerging cyber threats.

One pivotal aspect of linguistic interaction security lies in the encryption of digital communication. Encryption protects against unauthorized access, ensuring that linguistic data remains confidential and integral during transmission. As individuals share sensitive information through digital platforms, encryption algorithms prevent eavesdropping and unauthorized interception. End-to-end encryption, in particular, has gained prominence as a gold standard for securing linguistic interactions, providing a secure channel from the sender to the recipient without intermediaries having access to the unencrypted data. However, while encryption significantly enhances linguistic security, debates surrounding privacy concerns and lawful access to encrypted data persist, underscoring the delicate balance between safety and individual rights.

Incorporating artificial intelligence (AI) into language-based communication presents a range of security benefits and difficulties. Natural Language Processing (NLP) algorithms, a subset of AI, empower machines to comprehend and generate human language, revolutionizing how linguistic interactions occur in the digital realm. While AI-driven language security tools can examine enormous volumes of data to find irregularities and possible security threats, they also raise concerns about the ethical implications of AI in language processing. Issues such as bias in AI algorithms, unintended consequences of automated content moderation, and the potential misuse of AI for linguistic manipulation pose challenges that demand careful consideration in securing digital linguistic interactions.

Ethical issues heavily influence the conversation around the security of language interactions. Balancing the imperative to secure linguistic data with respect for privacy rights and freedom of expression requires a nuanced approach. Governments, technology companies, and individuals grapple with defining ethical boundaries in linguistic security practices, particularly in surveillance, data retention, and the trade-off between security and civil liberties. Finding the appropriate balance requires solid legal foundations, open policies, and a dedication to protecting human rights online.

The globalization of linguistic interactions in the digital age amplifies the complexity of securing communication across diverse languages and cultures. Language barriers, translation challenges, and cultural nuances introduce unique considerations in linguistic security. Digital platforms make it easier for people to communicate internationally, which makes language diversity in security measures necessary. Ensuring that linguistic security tools are practical across languages and cultures requires a commitment to inclusivity and an understanding of the linguistic intricacies that shape digital interactions on a global scale.

The dynamic nature of linguistic interactions in the digital realm also highlights the importance of user education and awareness. Individuals often unknowingly contribute to linguistic security vulnerabilities through practices such as weak password management, falling victim to phishing attacks, or sharing sensitive information on insecure platforms. Educating users about the risks associated with linguistic interactions and promoting best practices for digital communication hygiene empowers individuals to participate actively in the collective effort to enhance linguistic security.

Preserving Language Heritage in a Cyber Age

Language, a fundamental element of human culture and identity, has profoundly transformed in the digital era. The speed at which technology is being incorporated into our daily lives has completely changed how we communicate, which presents opportunities and difficulties for preserving linguistic diversity. This section explores the intricate interplay between language, technology, and cultural heritage, examining the impact of the cyber age on linguistic diversity, the role of digital tools in language preservation, the difficulties presented by language endangerment, and the ethical issues that arise in the quest to safeguard our linguistic heritage in an increasingly digitized world.

With the advent of the digital age, an era of unparalleled connectivity enables people from around the globe to engage in linguistic interactions easily. While this interconnectedness has facilitated the exchange of ideas and cultures, it also threatens linguistic diversity.

The dominance of a few major languages in the digital space can marginalize more minor languages, putting them at risk of extinction. The allure of global communication in widely spoken languages can overshadow the importance of preserving linguistic diversity, making it imperative for efforts to leverage technology in the service of language heritage preservation.

Digital tools and platforms offer promising avenues for documenting and revitalizing endangered languages. Creating online dictionaries, archives, and language learning applications has become instrumental in capturing and disseminating linguistic knowledge. Social media, blogs, and digital storytelling platforms provide spaces for communities to share and celebrate their languages, fostering a sense of pride and continuity. Additionally, machine translation and speech recognition technologies contribute to the preservation effort by facilitating the digitization of oral traditions and written texts, making them more accessible to a global audience.

Despite these opportunities, the challenge of language endangerment remains a pressing issue. Thousands of languages are at risk of disappearing due to globalization, urbanization, and the pervasive influence of dominant languages in the digital landscape. The digital divide further exacerbates this challenge, as communities with limited access to technology find themselves on the margins of the digital linguistic landscape. Coordinated efforts will be needed to make technology accessible and culturally sensitive to close this gap and enable underprivileged populations to take an active role in digitally preserving their language heritage.

The confluence of language preservation and the digital age raises several ethical questions. The commodification of language data, the potential exploitation of indigenous knowledge, and the risk of misrepresentation in digital archives raise ethical concerns that demand careful navigation. Collaborative and respectful partnerships between technologists, linguists, and communities are essential to ensure that digital language preservation efforts prioritize cultural sensitivity, informed consent, and the empowerment of linguistic communities rather than perpetuating digital colonialism.

The rise of artificial intelligence (AI) introduces opportunities and challenges in language preservation. While AI-driven tools can automate the transcription and translation of languages, enhancing efficiency in preservation efforts, they also pose risks related to accuracy, bias, and cultural appropriation. Striking a balance between the benefits of AI and the need for human expertise in linguistic preservation is crucial to avoid unintended consequences that could compromise the authenticity and integrity of language heritage.

Regarding language conservation, the digital era offers a forum for reviving languages in danger of extinction. Digital storytelling, online language courses, and collaborative platforms enable communities to preserve their languages and pass them on to future generations. Moreover, the digital medium allows for dynamic and evolving forms of expression, fostering the creation of new linguistic content that reflects the contemporary experiences of language communities.

One key consideration in the digital preservation of language heritage is the potential loss of linguistic depth and richness. As languages adapt to the constraints and opportunities of the digital medium, there is a risk of simplification and standardization that may dilute the nuances and intricacies of traditional linguistic forms. Balancing the need for accessibility and ease of communication with the preservation of linguistic diversity and complexity is a delicate task that requires thoughtful design and consideration in developing digital language tools.

The role of education in language preservation must be balanced, particularly in the context of the cyber age. Digital platforms offer innovative ways to integrate language learning into formal and informal educational settings, making language preservation an integral part of the curriculum. Language apps, online courses, and interactive digital resources provide learners with immersive experiences beyond traditional classroom settings, fostering a sense of connection to language heritage from an early age.

Community engagement is critical to effective language preservation initiatives in the digital age. Empowering communities to actively participate in the digital documentation and revitalization of their languages ensures that preservation initiatives are rooted in the lived experiences and aspirations of the people. The durability and applicability of digital language preservation initiatives are enhanced by cooperative strategies prioritizing local expertise and considering community feedback.

Balancing Connectivity with Privacy and Security

The world has shrunk to a global village in the era of unheard-of technology connectedness, erasing national, organizational, and individual borders and changing how people interact. While this connectivity has undeniably brought numerous benefits, it has also given rise to profound concerns about privacy and security. Striking a delicate balance between connectivity, privacy, and security is one of the most pressing challenges of our digital era. This section explores the intricate dynamics of this trilemma, delving into the evolution of connectivity, the implications for privacy and security, the role of emerging technologies, and the imperative of finding equilibrium in a rapidly evolving digital landscape.

The evolution of connectivity has been nothing short of revolutionary, transforming the world into an interconnected web of information and communication. On a never-before-seen scale, social media, mobile devices, and the internet have made collaborating, communicating, and obtaining information more accessible. The benefits of this connectivity are vast, ranging from economic growth and innovation to enhanced global communication and collaboration. However, this interconnectedness has also exposed individuals and organizations to new vulnerabilities, as the pervasiveness of digital communication creates an expansive attack surface for malicious actors seeking to exploit weaknesses in the digital infrastructure.

Privacy, once considered a fundamental aspect of personal freedom, has become increasingly elusive in the era of connectivity. The digital footprint left by individuals as they navigate online spaces has become a commodity, with personal data often harvested, analyzed, and monetized by corporations for targeted advertising and other purposes. Social media platforms, in particular, have become focal points for privacy concerns as users grapple with the trade-off between sharing personal information for social connectivity and safeguarding their privacy. The erosion of privacy in the digital age raises ethical questions about the boundaries between private and public spaces, prompting a critical examination of the societal implications of pervasive connectivity.

In contrast, security has become a top priority, given the prevalence of cyber threats and digital vulnerabilities. As connectivity increases, so does the surface area vulnerable to cyber attacks, ranging from data breaches and ransom ware attacks to sophisticated state-sponsored cyber espionage. The interconnectedness of critical infrastructure, such as energy grids and financial systems, amplifies the potential impact of cyber threats on national security. Strong cyber security is a difficult task that calls for a multipronged strategy that includes legislative frameworks, technology advancements, and user awareness. The difficulty is in putting security measures in place without sacrificing connectivity's advantages or violating people's right to privacy.

However, deploying AI in surveillance and predictive analysis also raises concerns about mass surveillance and the erosion of privacy. The IoT, connecting everyday devices to the internet, offers convenience and efficiency but introduces new vulnerabilities as these interconnected devices become potential targets for cyber attacks. Blockchain technology, known for its decentralized and tamper-resistant nature, holds promise for securing data and transactions, but its adoption faces challenges related to scalability and regulatory frameworks.

As we navigate the complex landscape of connectivity, privacy, and security, finding a balance becomes imperative to harness the benefits of the digital age while mitigating its risks. Legislation and regulatory frameworks play a crucial role in defining the boundaries of permissible practices and ensuring accountability in the digital realm. Maintaining equilibrium in regulatory strategies necessitates a sophisticated comprehension of the dynamic digital terrain and the ability to modify legal structures to tackle new issues.

User awareness and digital literacy are pillars of a balanced relationship between connectivity, privacy, and security. It is essential to empower individuals with the knowledge and tools to protect their digital identities and make informed choices about privacy settings. Educational initiatives that promote responsible digital citizenship, cyber security best practices, and an understanding of the implications of online activities contribute to a more resilient and privacy-conscious digital society.

Technologies known as privacy-enhancing technologies, or PETs, provide creative ways to protect privacy without sacrificing the advantages of connectivity. People can manage the disclosure of their data while still engaging in digital interactions thanks to strategies like differential privacy, anonymization, and encryption. By incorporating PETs into digital platforms and services, users may navigate the digital landscape with more assurance that their data is secure and private.

Adopting a security-first mentality is essential for tackling the difficulties associated with connectivity at the organizational level. A thorough security strategy must include implementing strong cyber security measures, frequent risk assessments, and developing an employee culture that values cyber security. Organizations must also be transparent about their data practices, providing clear information to users about how their data will be used, stored, and protected.

In the national and international security realm, collaborative efforts are essential to address the cross-border nature of cyber threats. Information sharing, joint cyber security exercises, and developing international norms and standards contribute to a more secure and interconnected global digital ecosystem. Establishing principles of responsible state behavior in cyberspace through diplomatic initiatives can lay the groundwork for fostering international collaboration and confidence.

The ethical dimensions of balancing connectivity, privacy, and security underscore the importance of accountability and responsible innovation. Technology developers, policymakers, and organizations are responsible for prioritizing ethical considerations in designing, deploying, and regulating digital technologies. Ethical principles such as transparency, fairness, and respect for human rights should guide the development of new technologies and the formulation of policies that govern their use.

Chapter X

Future Trends
in Language Alchemy

The Evolving Role of Language in Technological Advancements

Alongside technology, language, the foundation of human communication, has experienced a radical metamorphosis. As technology continues to shape and redefine our daily lives, the role of language in this digital landscape becomes increasingly significant. This section examines the changing relationship between language and technology, looking at how technological advances influence and are influenced by language. From the earliest programming languages to the complexities of natural language processing and the emergence of voice-activated assistants, the symbiotic relationship between language and technology underscores the dynamic nature of our digital era.

The interconnection between language and technology can be traced back to the development of programming languages. In the mid-20th century, as computers emerged as powerful tools for computation, the need for a standardized means of communicating instructions to these machines became evident. This created programming languages such as Fortran, COBOL, and Lisp. These languages were designed to bridge the gap between human thought processes and machine execution, enabling programmers to effectively communicate complex algorithms and commands to computers. The syntax and semantics of programming languages became a unique form of speech, laying the groundwork for the evolution of computational linguistics.

The intersection of language and technology took a significant leap forward with the advent of natural language processing (NLP).NLP is an area of artificial intelligence that specializes in enabling machines to understand, interpret, and generate human language in a meaningful and contextually aware way. This technological advancement represents a convergence of linguistic theories, computer science, and cognitive psychology. NLP applications range from language translation and sentiment analysis to chatbots and voice recognition systems. The ability of machines to comprehend and respond to human language has transformed user interactions with technology. Still, it has opened new frontiers in healthcare, customer service, and education.

Machine Translation (MT) is a prominent example of how language has driven technological advancements—the the effort to reduce language barriers and promote international communication led to early machine translation efforts. However, the advent of statistical and neural machine translation models marked a paradigm shift in language technology. Google Translate, powered by neural machine translation, exemplifies the progress in automatic language translation. This technology relies on sophisticated algorithms that analyze multilingual data to generate contextually accurate translations. The evolution of MT demonstrates the advancement of language technology and raises questions about preserving linguistic nuances and cultural context in automated translations.

Voice-activated virtual assistants, like Google Assistant, Alexa, and Siri, are prime examples of how language and technology are combined in our day-to-day activities. These assistants rely on sophisticated speech recognition and natural language understanding algorithms to process and respond to verbal commands. Humanizing these interactions—where users converse with technology—highlights how language is a conduit between people and machines. As these voice-activated assistants evolve, the challenges of enhancing their linguistic capabilities, understanding user intent, and maintaining privacy become increasingly prominent.

Integrating language technology into our daily routines extends beyond virtual assistants, including smart devices, search engines, and social media platforms. Search engines, powered by complex algorithms and natural language processing; enable users to access information by entering queries in natural language. Social media platforms leverage language technology for content moderation, sentiment analysis, and personalized content recommendations. Applying language models in these settings raises moral questions about prejudice, privacy, and possible abuse of linguistic data.

In the realm of education, technology has redefined language learning and literacy. Language apps, interactive e-books, and online courses utilize technology to provide immersive language experiences. Augmented or virtual reality gamification enhances language learning by creating engaging and interactive environments. The evolving role of technology in language education not only transforms the methods of instruction but also democratizes access to language learning resources, breaking down traditional barriers to linguistic proficiency.

The impact of language on technology is not confined to the realm of user interfaces and computational linguistics. The vocabulary we choose to discuss and characterize technology affects how the public views it, how policies are decided, and how society views innovation. The terminology surrounding emerging technologies, such as artificial intelligence, block chain, and the Internet of Things, contributes to the public discourse on these advancements' ethical, social, and economic implications. The power dynamics embedded in the language used to describe technology also shape public trust, regulatory frameworks, and the responsible development of technological solutions.

As language and technology evolve, the challenges and opportunities that arise demand careful consideration. The moral use of language technology poses a big problem, especially regarding justice and bias. Language models, trained on vast datasets reflective of societal biases, may perpetuate and amplify existing prejudices. It takes a coordinated effort to provide inclusive datasets, use morally sound algorithms, and create open assessment frameworks to address language technology bias. The responsible deployment of language technology also involves navigating issues of privacy, consent, and the potential misuse of linguistic data, necessitating robust ethical guidelines and regulatory frameworks.

The cultural and linguistic implications of technology's influence on language are another aspect that warrants attention. As communication becomes increasingly mediated by digital platforms and standardized language models, there is a risk of homogenizing linguistic diversity. The challenge lies in preserving the richness of languages, dialects, and linguistic nuances in the face of globalized communication. Efforts to develop inclusive language technologies that respect and reflect the diversity of human expression are essential in mitigating the potential negative impact on linguistic and cultural heritage.

In the future, rising themes like multimodal interfaces, explainable AI, and the incorporation of emotion recognition into language technology will probably influence language and technology. Explainable AI aims to enhance transparency and accountability in machine decision-making processes, ensuring that users can understand and trust the outcomes generated by AI systems. Multimodal interfaces, which combine language with visuals, gestures, and other modalities, offer new dimensions for human-computer interaction. Emotion recognition technology, when integrated with language processing, can create emotionally intelligent interfaces, enabling technology to understand better and respond to users' emotional states.

Multimodal Communication: Integration of Language and Visuals

Combining language and images has become a potent and dynamic force in human communication. This integration, known as multimodal communication, reflects the recognition that language alone may not capture human expression's full richness and complexity. In a world saturated with images, videos, and digital interfaces, the combination of linguistic and visual elements has become central to how we convey meaning, share information, and engage with one another. This section examines the complex field of multimodal communication. It looks at its historical origins, the cognitive foundations of language and images, the influence of digital technologies, and the implications for various industries, including advertising, education, and user interface design.

Instead of being a relatively new development, multimodal communication is an essential feature of human connection with a long history. From ancient cave paintings to medieval illuminated manuscripts, humans have long combined visual elements with language to communicate narratives, convey emotions, and share knowledge. The Renaissance saw the development of printing technology, which marked a transformative moment, allowing for the mass production of books that seamlessly integrated text and illustrations. Over time, the fields of art, literature, and design evolved to explore the interplay between language and visuals, setting the stage for the contemporary era of multimodal communication.

The cognitive foundations of multimodal communication are rooted in how our brains process and make sense of information. Research in cognitive science suggests that humans are inherently multisensory beings able to simultaneously perceive and integrate data from various modalities. Language and visuals activate different brain regions, and their combination can enhance comprehension, retention, and emotional engagement. Allan Paivio's dual-coding theory states that when knowledge is integrated with verbal and non-verbal information processing channels, it is represented more robustly and abundantly.

Language is a symbolic system for encoding and conveying abstract concepts in multimodal communication, while visuals provide concrete and immediate representations. This complementary relationship between the abstract and the concrete allows for a more holistic understanding of information. For example, a presentation combining spoken words with relevant images is likely more effective in conveying a message than either modality alone. Language and pictures enhance our cognitive abilities and facilitate how our brains naturally process information.

A new era of digital technologies has brought about multimodal communication, fundamentally reshaping how we create, consume, and interact with information. The rise of the internet, social media, and digital content platforms has democratized the production and distribution of multimodal content. Users now have the tools to seamlessly integrate interactive features, movies, photos, and text to create a rich tapestry of communication. Mainly, social media platforms have developed into centers of multimodal expression, where people utilize text, images, emoticons, and multimedia information to share experiences, viewpoints, and tales.

One of the transformative aspects of digital multimodal communication is the shift from passive consumption to active participation. Users are not merely receivers of information but also contributors to the multimodal discourse. Platforms like Instagram, TikTok, and YouTube empower individuals to tell their stories through a combination of visuals and language, fostering a sense of digital agency and creativity. The interactive nature of digital multimodal communication has profound implications for user engagement, brand storytelling, and the democratization of expression.

Multimodal communication is essential for improving the educational experience. Text-based educational tools that incorporate diagrams, multimedia, and images accommodate a variety of learning preferences and foster comprehension. Digital textbooks, interactive simulations, and online courses leverage the power of multimodal communication to create immersive and engaging learning environments. Platforms for educational technology, including Coursera and Khan Academy, exemplify how integrating language and visuals can democratize access to knowledge and provide personalized learning experiences globally.

The integration of language and visuals has also transformed the advertising and marketing landscape. Advertisers leverage the power of storytelling, combining compelling narratives with visually striking images or videos to create memorable and persuasive campaigns. The introduction of social media advertising highlights the significance of creating visually appealing material that can stand out in a congested online environment. Brands understand that a compelling advertisement requires a careful balance between linguistic elements that convey a message and visuals that evoke emotions and resonate with the target audience.

User interface design represents another domain where multimodal communication plays a pivotal role. Designing digital interfaces, whether for websites, mobile apps, or virtual reality environments, involves carefully considering how language and visuals work together to create an intuitive and user-friendly experience. Icons, buttons, and infographics contribute to the visual language of interfaces, complementing textual elements and guiding users through interactive experiences. As technology advances, integrating voice commands, gestures, and augmented reality further expands the possibilities for multimodal interfaces that seamlessly blend language and visuals.

However, there are drawbacks to the widespread use of multimodal communication in the digital age, especially regarding information overload and visual literacy. The constant stream of images, videos, and text in digital spaces can overwhelm individuals, making it challenging to discern meaningful content from noise. To successfully navigate the complicated world of online information, one must possess digital literacy abilities, including the ability to assess and comprehend multimodal communications critically. The role of education in fostering visual literacy—teaching individuals to analyze and create visuals in conjunction with language—is crucial in equipping individuals with the skills needed to navigate the multimodal digital landscape.

Ethical considerations also come to the forefront in multimodal communication, particularly concerning the manipulation of visuals and the potential for misinformation. Deepfakes, altered photos, and deceptive visual content threaten the legitimacy of information in the digital sphere. The ethical use of visuals, transparency in content creation, and media literacy efforts are essential in addressing these challenges and maintaining the integrity of multimodal communication.

Looking ahead, the future of multimodal communication holds exciting possibilities and challenges. As technology advances, immersive experiences integrating virtual reality, augmented reality, and holography with language will likely become more prevalent. The emergence of artificial intelligence (AI)-)-powered instruments that produce text, image, and video information in multiple formats prompt inquiries regarding the possibility of automating creative expression. Balancing the advantages of automation with the preservation of human creativity and intentionality becomes a key consideration.

Emerging Frontiers and Innovations in Language Technology

The field of language technology is constantly changing because of the rapid growth of technology, creating new opportunities and possibilities previously unimaginable. Language technology has developed into a dynamic field at the nexus of linguistics, artificial intelligence, and computational science. Examples of its applications include sentiment analysis, conversational bots, natural language processing, and machine translation. This section explores the emerging frontiers and innovations in language technology, examining the transformative impact of recent developments, the challenges accompanying these advancements, and the implications for diverse applications ranging from healthcare and business to education and beyond.

One of the groundbreaking frontiers in language technology is developing and refining natural language processing (NLP) models. Natural language processing (NLP), a branch of artificial intelligence, aims to enable robots to produce, understand, and interpret human language in a semantically meaningful and contextually aware manner. NLP has been entirely transformed by recent developments in deep learning, especially the emergence of transformer-based models. Models like OpenAI's GPT-3 (Generative Pre-trained Transformer 3) showcase the capabilities of large-scale language models, demonstrating the capacity to generate coherent and contextually relevant text that mirrors human-like linguistic proficiency. These models have applications in various domains, from content generation and language translation to code completion and chatbot interactions.

Machine translation, a longstanding challenge in language technology, has seen remarkable progress with the advent of neural machine translation (NMT) models. These models leverage deep neural networks to improve the accuracy and fluency of automated translations between languages. Google's Neural Machine Translation (GNMT) and other state-of-the-art systems have narrowed the gap between human and machine translation capabilities. The ability to generate contextually accurate translations has profound implications for global communication, cross-cultural collaboration, and the dissemination of information across linguistic barriers. However, challenges persist in ensuring that machine translations capture the nuances and cultural subtleties embedded in human languages.

Sentiment analysis, another frontier in language technology, focuses on the automated extraction of emotional tones and attitudes from text. Numerous industries have benefited from this breakthrough, including social media monitoring, customer feedback analysis, and brand perception evaluation. Sentiment analysis models, often powered by machine learning algorithms, can categorize text as positive, negative, or neutral, providing valuable insights into public opinion and sentiment trends. Creating models that can effectively read the intricacies of human emotions while taking sarcasm, cultural context, and other linguistic details that may affect sentiment into account is a challenging task.

Conversational agents, commonly known as chatbots or virtual assistants, represent a prominent frontier in language technology with transformative implications for human-computer interaction. These agents leverage natural language understanding and generation to engage in text or voice-based conversations with users. Companies like Apple, Amazon, and Microsoft have integrated conversational agents into their products and services, from smartphone virtual assistants to chatbots for customer support. The challenge in developing effective conversational agents lies in creating models that can understand user intent, respond contextually, and exhibit conversational coherence that mirrors human interactions.

The emergence of multimodal language models represents a fusion of linguistic and visual elements, opening new frontiers in understanding and generating content. Models like CLIP (Contrastive Language-Image Pre-training) and DALL-E, developed by OpenAI, demonstrate the capacity to understand and generate content based on textual and visual inputs. This multimodal method has consequences for content production, picture captioning, and accessibility for people with visual impairments. Nonetheless, obstacles still exist in guaranteeing the moral application of multimodal models, steering clear of prejudices, and encouraging inclusivity in portraying varied language and visual content.

Language technology is making significant strides in healthcare, contributing to advancements in clinical documentation, medical research, and patient care. Natural language processing facilitates extracting valuable information from medical records, enabling clinicians and researchers to analyze large datasets for insights into disease patterns, treatment outcomes, and epidemiological trends. Chatbots and virtual health assistants offer personalized health information, appointment scheduling, and medication reminders, enhancing patient engagement and healthcare accessibility. But protecting the confidentiality and security of private health information remains a critical consideration in adopting language technology in healthcare settings.

Business and commerce are also experiencing the transformative impact of language technology, particularly in customer service, marketing, and data analytics. Chatbots deployed in customer support functions can provide immediate assistance, answer queries, and facilitate transactions, improving efficiency and user satisfaction. Sentiment analysis tools help businesses gauge customer feedback, track brand perception, and identify areas for improvement. Moreover, language models contribute to the automation of content creation, enabling the generation of product descriptions, marketing copy, and social media posts. Finding a middle ground between automation and the maintenance of actual human contact is challenging, ensuring that language technology augments rather than diminishes the human element in commercial dealings.

Education is undergoing a revolution with language technology integration, offering innovative solutions for language learning, literacy development, and personalized instruction. Language apps and online platforms leverage natural language processing to provide interactive and adaptive language learning experiences. Automated feedback systems analyze written assignments, offering instant suggestions for improvement and facilitating the learning process. Virtual tutors and conversational agents assist language learners in practicing and honing their speaking skills. Reducing the digital divide and making language technology tools available to students from various socioeconomic backgrounds are complex tasks.

The ethical considerations surrounding language technology are becoming increasingly prominent as these innovations permeate various aspects of society. Issues such as bias in language models, the responsible use of automated content generation, and the potential for misuse in disseminating misinformation raise questions about the ethical deployment of language technology. Transparent and inclusive development practices, ongoing scrutiny of algorithms for biases, and incorporating ethical considerations in the design and implementation of language technology are essential for mitigating these ethical challenges.

The language technology field has excellent opportunities and challenging obstacles in store for the future. The development of explainable AI aims to enhance transparency and accountability in language models, ensuring that users can understand and trust the decisions made by these systems. Multimodal interfaces, combining language with visuals, gestures, and other modalities, offer new dimensions for human-computer interaction. Emotion recognition technology, when integrated with language processing, can create emotionally intelligent interfaces, enabling technology to understand better and respond to users' emotional states.

Conclusion

In the last chapters of "Language Alchemy: Bridging the Gap Between Humans and Machines Through Language," the digital era is shaped by the transforming potential of linguistic integration, which is shown as a critical factor. The historical roots of language, the effects of the digital revolution, and the changing field of language technology are all covered in this examination of language in the context of human-machine interaction.

As the book delves into the challenges and opportunities of linguistic diversity in a globalized digital landscape, it sheds light on the delicate balance between connectivity and the preservation of cultural and linguistic heritage. The rise of online language communities and the emergence of Internet English serve as testaments to the dynamic nature of language, evolving in response to the digital ecosystem.

By demystifying the basic concepts of language technology, such as natural language processing (NLP) models and algorithms, readers can understand the complex mechanics that underlie machines' ability to comprehend, interpret, and produce human language. Ethical considerations in language technology further prompt reflection on the responsible development and deployment of these transformative tools.

Human-machine interaction through language takes center stage, exploring the role of virtual assistants, chat bots, and voice-activated devices in seamlessly integrating language into everyday life. The book focuses on the mutually beneficial link between language and artificial intelligence, emphasizing how these innovations improve human relationships and change how people communicate.

Cultural preservation in the digital age emerges as a pressing concern, prompting discussions on digital initiatives for language revitalization and the impact of digital platforms on minority languages. The investigation of language acquisition in the digital age highlights how internet platforms can revolutionize education, literacy, and knowledge sharing.

The fusion of language and visual elements, from memes to graphic language, unveils the richness and complexity of modern communication. The book navigates the challenges and nuances of visual communication, acknowledging its role in shaping cultural narratives and linguistic trends.

Addressing cyber security concerns, the book advocates for securing linguistic interactions in the digital realm while preserving language heritage. It emphasizes how crucial it is to balance privacy, security, and connectivity, acknowledging the risks and safety measures in our language interactions.

Looking toward the future, the book explores emerging trends in language alchemy, predicting the continued evolution of language in tandem with technological advancements. Multimodal communication, the integration of language with visuals, and other innovations in language technology offer a sneak peek at the fascinating opportunities that wait.

Finally, "Language Alchemy" ask readers to consider language's significant influence on the changing dynamic between people and machines. It underscores the dynamic interplay between linguistic diversity, technological innovation, and cultural preservation, leaving readers with a heightened appreciation for the transformative potential of language in the digital age. The book serves not only as a comprehensive exploration of language alchemy but also as a catalyst for ongoing conversations about the future of language and its integral role in our ever-evolving digital landscape.

Thank you for buying and reading/listening to our book.
If you found this book useful/helpful please take a few minutes
and leave a review on the platform where you purchased our book.
Your feedback matters greatly to us.

www.ingramcontent.com/pod-product-compliance
Lightning Source LLC
Chambersburg PA
CBHW071511150726
48000CB00002B/541